# WHAT ARE THEY SAYING ABOUT
# SOCIAL SIN?

# What Are They Saying About Social Sin?

*Mark O'Keefe, O.S.B.*

PAULIST PRESS
*New York/Mahwah*

Library of Congress Cataloging-in-Publication Data

O'Keefe, Mark, 1956–
    What are they saying about social sin?/by Mark O'Keefe.
      p.  cm.
    Includes bibliographical references.
    ISBN 0-8091-3161-7
    1. Sin.  2. Sociology, Christian (Catholic)  3. Catholic Church—
Doctrines.  I. Title.  II. Title: Social sin.
    BX1753.046     1990
    241'.3—dc20                            89-78399
                                                 CIP

Published by Paulist Press
997 Macarthur Boulevard
Mahwah, NJ 07430

# Contents

# Introduction

In 1973, psychiatrist Karl Menninger asked the question, *Whatever Became of Sin?*, suggesting that modern society has lost its sense of sin and moral responsibility.[1] There is no doubt that the understanding of sin has been in flux in Christian theology and in popular practice in the years immediately before and after the Second Vatican Council. At the same time, however, the recognition of sin has been and remains a central component of Christian experience, self-understanding, and theology. What, for example, does a doctrine of "salvation" and the identification of Jesus Christ as "Savior" mean independent of a doctrine of sin?

For Roman Catholics, at least before the Second Vatican Council, the confessional "box" was the great symbol of human sinfulness and the need for repentance and penance. Good Catholics faithfully and regularly examined their consciences for violations of the commandments and of church law and confessed these sinful infractions to the priest as the witness of the church. Many can recall the lines of penitents waiting silently in and even outside Catholic churches on Saturday afternoons as the faithful devoutly confessed their guilt before God and the church.

In the late 1960s and into the 1970s, there developed in Christian theology and, to a lesser extent, in Christian consciousness in general an appreciation that the reality of sin was

1

somehow broader than those personal sins which had been the traditional subject of the sacrament of penance. Theologians, reflecting in a renewed fashion on scripture and tradition as well as on human experience, came to see that sin is also a social phenomenon. It became clear that sin is more than personal acts of dishonesty or slander or unchastity.

More particularly, as ministers and theologians reflected on the injustices confronting the poor in the third world and in modern, urbanized, and industrialized societies, they began to name these injustices as "sin." The evil experienced by the poor was not "evil" in the same manner in which suffering caused by natural disasters is an evil. Rather, the suffering of the poor came to be understood as somehow "sinful"—that is, the evil was caused by social factors rooted in human institutions and ultimately, though perhaps indirectly, in human choices. Suddenly good and sincere people began to see the possibility that they might themselves be implicated in the institutions which caused the suffering of others. This understanding of sin as social, as rooted in social institutions, and as implicating persons who had no intention of inflicting harm on others came to be known as a theology of social sin.

The present work attempts to provide a critical overview of what theologians are saying about social sin. Though the notion of social sin has gained wide acceptance in Christian theological circles, there have been relatively few sustained and systematic studies of its foundations. The present work will examine a number of the major discussions of social sin in the effort to identify the foundations thus far laid.

The first chapter will place the contemporary discussion of social sin within the context of the Christian tradition's understanding of sin. In particular it will identify evidence of the long-standing recognition of sin as a social phenomenon in the tradition. Further, it will suggest factors which contributed both to the privatizing trend in the theology of sin and, more recently, to its renewal. Finally the first chapter will address the question of how radically the contemporary theology of sin reinterprets the traditional Catholic theology of sin in light of the relationship between personal and social sin.

The second chapter will examine various terms used by contemporary theologians to denote the social dimensions of sin. By examining terms and their definitions as well as various metaphors suggested to denote the experience of sin as social, it is hoped that a greater appreciation can be gained about the reality to which these terms and metaphors are directed.

The third chapter will look more directly at the theological and especially sociological foundations of a theology of social sin. It is precisely sociology which enables theologians to understand how sin can become rooted, embodied, and perpetuated in social institutions. Understanding these social factors is of course the foundation of attempting to overcome and transform them.

Building on the foundation laid in the third chapter, chapter four will suggest in more direct fashion "how social sin works," using racism as an example. More particularly, it will examine the question of how social sin impacts moral deliberation itself. Finally, the chapter will address the difficult problem of individual responsibility for social sin.

A fifth chapter will examine the distinctive contribution to a theology of social sin offered by the cognitional theory and the notion of conversion of Bernard Lonergan. Those theologians who seek to build on the thought of Lonergan have offered significant contributions to the development of a theology of social sin and conversion. The discussion in chapter five will lead then in the final chapter to a discussion of social conversion.

The final chapter will suggest the "shape" of an authentic social conversion. It will then offer some important "strategies" for social conversion, devoting particular emphasis to the church's distinctive role. Finally, the sixth chapter will discuss the problem of the relationship of personal conversion and social transformation which seems—naturally enough— to parallel the discussion of the relationship between personal and social sin.

The social reality of sin is a particular emphasis of liberation theologies, especially Latin American and feminist theologies; thus, a special effort will be made in the present study to indicate their distinctive perspectives. Despite differing emphases and perspectives, however, there seems to be a more basic consistency in the discussion of social sin which crosses the lines of different theological methods and perspectives.

I am grateful to those who aided me in arriving at the final form of this work. Rev. Cyprian Davis, O.S.B., Br. Edward Linton, O.S.B., and Rev. Adrian Correa offered helpful comments on sections of the work while in preparation. My colleague, Rev. Mark Ciganovich, O.Carm., read the entire manuscript and offered some invaluable suggestions.

I dedicate this book to my parents, William J. and Tomiyo O'Keefe.

# 1. Social Sin and the Tradition

The Christian tradition in general and the Roman Catholic tradition in particular have always, in some form, recognized the social aspects of sin. This remains true despite the fact that the Roman Catholic theology of sin, in the several hundred years before the Second Vatican Council, was largely characterized by individualism and by a concern for private, personal acts. This is not the place to develop an historical analysis of the Christian theology of sin;[1] however, identifying some stages in the appreciation of sin's social aspects will help to place the contemporary discussion in an adequate context. The present chapter, therefore, will provide a brief overview of consistent elements in the tradition which point to the social aspects of sin, and it will suggest some reasons for the decline of the appreciation of these social elements. After a brief summary of the resulting understanding of sin in the pre-Vatican II manuals of moral theology, the chapter will indicate several factors that have led to the retrieval of the tradition's appreciation of sin as a social reality. A final section will examine how "radically" contemporary discussions of social sin reinterpret the traditional concept of sin particularly in regard to the relationship between social and personal sin.

## Reclaiming the Tradition

That sin has social aspects was readily apparent to biblical authors, both in Hebrew and Christian scriptures.[2] Scripture scholars have long argued that the first eleven chapters of the book of Genesis, the narrative that runs from Adam and Eve through the flood to the tower of Babel, demonstrate the social effects of sin and perhaps the historical growth of sin.[3] In the Hebrew scriptures, the reality of sin is understood in the social context of the covenant between God and the community of Israel. Sin affects the entire community, and it is the entire community which faces the judgment of God and is called to repentance. In fact, it is relatively late in the Hebrew scriptures that a clear notion of individual responsibility begins to co-exist with the earlier self-understanding of corporate solidarity.

The prophets are rather obviously calling the people to repent of sinful business practices and unjust treatment of the poor and helpless which violate their covenant responsibilities to other persons and to God. The prophets condemn not only individual unjust actions but prevailing attitudes. Even more fundamentally, however, they denounce these injustices as they permeate political structures, economic relationships, the prevailing customs and the accepted mores, and the legal institutions.[4] Sin, therefore, is not merely the injustice (and thus violation of the covenant) of one person but an unfaithfulness to the covenant which permeates the community.

In the New Testament, the social reality of sin is rather clearly reflected in Paul's discussion of the "world" and of the "reign of sin." The spirit of this world and its rulers are in opposition to God (1 Cor 2:8, 12). Sin is said to "reign" in this world (Rom 5:21; 6:14) and "enslaves" humanity (Rom 6:6, 17, 20; Gal 3:22). It becomes clear that, for Paul, sin is larger than personal choice and in some significant way is rooted in the social world.[5]

The Johannine literature makes frequent pejorative use of the term "the world" (cf. Jn 12:31; 14:30; 16:11), and the opposition between the world and God's work in Christ is more prominent than in the Pauline literature. Satan is the "prince of this world" (Jn 12:21; 14:30; 16:11), and the world is identified with hostility to the work of Christ. Thus, the Johannine literature, like the earlier works of both the Hebrew and Christian scriptures, manifests an awareness that sin is a social reality, a context in which individual persons find themselves and in which they act.[6]

The recognition of the social aspects of sin was continued by the early church in its communal celebrations of penance. Serious, public sins required public confession and public penance before the church. Despite the rise of the practice of private confession after the sixth century, the sacrament of reconciliation, in whatever form, continues to display the appreciation of sin's social aspects. The penitent confesses to the priest precisely because his or her sin has damaged at least the Christian community represented in the sacrament by its official minister. In this context, the social effects of personal sin are understood to be manifest directly in those sinful actions which cause positive harm to another (e.g. stealing, murder) and indirectly through the fact that personal sin renders the Christian unable to be a channel of grace to others.

The doctrine of original sin, moreover, clearly understands sin to have a power beyond the individual. It attests to a certain "solidarity in sin," a universality to human sinfulness—at least in its effects and ongoing power to lead to further sin. A clear distinction has been made—and must be made—between the social aspects of personal (mortal) sin and original sin; still, original sin attests to a mystery of sin that transcends the individual. Sin is, to some degree and in some form, a reality which can be "inherited," into which one can be born.

## A Trend Toward Individualism

Despite the consistent though largely implicit witness to sin's social aspects in the Bible, in liturgical practice, and in the doctrine of original sin, it must be noted that the recognition of sin as a social reality was largely hidden in the centuries preceding the Second Vatican Council.[7] An individualistic trend emerged that identified sin almost exclusively as an individual and almost private matter. Sin came to be understood solely as a personal and virtually private act.

A number of factors can be suggested to account for the privatizing of the notion of sin. Some have attributed this growing individualism to the practice of private auricular confession, introduced in the sixth century by the Irish monks.[8] With serious sin no longer confessed before the assembled community with the imposition of public penance —replaced by a private confession to a priest with the imposition of a private penance—sin itself came to be understood as a private matter with only a tenuous connection with the wider community. The rise of nominalism in the late middle ages furthered the privatizing trend by placing greater emphasis on the uniqueness of the particular individual and thus on individual acts and laws.

The growing attention to sinful *acts*, focusing attention on personal and individual sin, was codified in the Roman Catholic tradition with the Council of Trent's decree that every mortal sin be confessed according to number and kind. The manuals of moral theology in use in Catholic seminaries in the late nineteenth and early twentieth centuries furthered the almost exclusive emphasis on sin as a private act through their attempt to identify clear and precise criteria by which the confessor could act as judge in the confessional. As Patrick McCormick has recently argued, correlative to the image of priest as judge is the image of penitent as criminal and sin as an individual crime.[9] It has been argued that neo-scholastic theology itself was characterized by an individualistic anthropology which resulted naturally in an individualistic theology of sin.[10]

The privatistic view of sin seems related as well to an individualism and privatism in Christian spirituality and piety prevalent in the Catholic Church before the Second Vatican Council. Grace itself was popularly understood to be operative almost exclusively within individual souls in order to move them to pious acts.[11] The range and goal of the spiritual life was popularly understood as the salvation of one's individual soul. In light of such a piety, it is not surprising that one's understanding of sin would likewise be individualistic and privatistic.

**Individual Sin in the Manuals**

The individualistic trend in the understanding of sin is apparent in the discussion of sin offered by the manuals of moral theology. These were the textbooks used in Roman Catholic seminaries and the reference works for priests in their confessional practice in the two hundred years before the Second Vatican Council. The manualist presentation of sin is therefore the understanding which guided teaching and practice throughout the church—an understanding which is shaped by the purpose of the manuals in training priests to be judges in the confessional. The present section offers a summary of the understanding of sin as it appears in the manuals. The summary does not intend to be comprehensive but rather to focus on the individualistic emphasis of the manualist perspective as an instance of the trend noted in the previous section.

The popular little manual by Jone and Adelman defines sin succinctly as "the free transgression of a divine law."[12] The manual by Henry Davis defines sin as "a morally bad human act, a privation of some obligatory good, a deflection from the order of right reason, and therefore from the law of God."[13] The emphasis in both definitions is clearly on individual human acts and laws (the discussion of which precedes the discussion of sin in both manuals). Given the history outlined above and the close connection which had arisen between moral theology and canon law (Jone and Adelman were canon lawyers), this emphasis is not surprising. McCormick's claim, mentioned above, that sin was viewed according to the model of crime is apparent.

The focus of the manuals on the individual who is sinning and on his or her discrete action is further highlighted by the conditions identified as necessary for mortal sin: grave matter, full knowledge, and free consent. True sin is thus committed when a gravely evil action is performed by an individual with sufficient knowledge and freedom. Any other form of sin (i.e. venial or original sin) is sin "by analogy." Therefore, though sins may have evil effects or consequences in the social world, the consequent evil and its lingering presence is not truly sin but precisely an effect of an individual's sin.

The emphasis on the individual sinner and his or her freely chosen action continues the individualizing trend outlined above. In examining one's conscience for the presence of sin, the penitent looked exclusively at his or her own freely chosen actions. The examination for participation in wider contexts of evil was not undertaken. One could, for example, recognize and confess an action motivated by greed but fail to recognize one's collaboration in economic practices and structures which offered material benefits to the penitent but at grievous cost to other (unseen) persons. A slaveowner "of good conscience" could quite conceivably recognize his or her

cruelty to an individual slave but remain completely inatten-
tive to the evil in the institution of slavery itself.

The manuals were quite aware that various factors could
mitigate responsibility by lessening the individual's freedom
or knowledge. The penitent could, for example, be sincerely
ignorant of any evil in an action which he or she had undertaken. As long as the ignorance itself was not freely chosen,
the person would not be guilty of true sin. The action would
then be *objectively* evil but the person would not be *subjec-
tively* culpable.

There is no doubt that the ability to distinguish between
objective wrongdoing ("material sin") and subjective culpability ("formal sin") in this manner is important to any moral
analysis. There is, after all, a clear moral difference between
killing by accident and killing with prior deliberation. An
over-emphasis on such possible mitigating factors seems,
however, to have played a role in blinding people to the social
dimensions of sin. It is often difficult enough to determine if I
truly acted with "full knowledge" and "full freedom" when
choosing to perform an evil action. The complexity of determining personal involvement and complicity in *social* evils is,
however, even more difficult. In the face of the complexity of
one's participation in various social interrelationships, it is
relatively easy to assume that mitigating factors have hindered
one's ability to know that one was an accomplice to social evil
and that one could have played a part in overcoming the evil.
Obviously, the vastness and the intricacy of social structures
and an individual's ability to understand one's part in them
can, in fact, mitigate responsibility for participation in social
evils. At the same time, however, excessive or even exclusive
attention to such mitigating factors seems to have contributed
further to the individualizing trend in the understanding of
sin manifested in the manuals.[14]

**Contemporary State of the Question**

The appreciation of the social aspects of sin has been revived in the years immediately before and certainly after the Second Vatican Council. A number of developments may be suggested as contributing factors in this renewed appreciation.

First is the development of Roman Catholic biblical scholarship in this century which has made the scriptural data more available to Roman Catholic theologians reflecting on sin. Thus, the prophetic denunciations of sin as a social reality, the Pauline concern for the "reign of sin," and the Johannine denunciation of "the world" have been brought to bear on the renewed theology of sin. In conjunction with the renewal of dogmatic theology, Catholic biblical studies have focused new attention on the social dimensions of salvation itself and of the kingdom of God.

Second, the renewal of a general theology of sin in the wider context of the renewal of Catholic moral theology, now more attentive to biblical perspectives, has moved away from an exclusive attention to acts, giving relatively more attention to sin as a stance, state, or orientation.[15] Fundamental option theory in particular moves the discussion of sin away from an exclusive focus on individual human acts and the conditions for assessing responsibility for each discrete act. The renewed theology of sin has, furthermore, been more attentive to the insights of psychology—including depth and social psychology—in regard to the various external and social influences on personal responsibility for sin. A greater attention to experience has also led to an appreciation that the experience of sin includes not only a sense of personal responsibility and wrongdoing but also the experience of sinfulness impinging on the person as if from outside, tempting the person to sin.[16] This renewed appreciation of sin's social dimension is further reflected in the church's contemporary liturgical practice of the communal celebration of the sacrament of reconciliation.

A third development in the renewed appreciation of sin as a social reality has been the contemporary effort to renew the theology of original sin. While continuing to recognize the internal effects of original sin on the individual, contemporary approaches to original sin (at least since Piet Schoonenberg's discussion of the "sin of the world" in the early 1960s) have devoted greater attention to its external, social effects. It must be noted once again that original sin, personal sin and "social sin" must be adequately distinguished; but the renewed interest in each has highlighted the social dimensions of sin and its effects.

Fourth is an increased attention in Catholic social thought to injustices as they become embodied in institutions, structures, and systems. This emphasis has held an important place in official Catholic social teaching since Pope Leo XIII.[17] Political and socio-economic relationships and structures have become more complex in the modern world, and it has become increasingly clear that efforts to help the poor and oppressed are blocked not so much by the ill-will of greedy individuals but by the embodiment of evil and its effects in established relationships and structures. This recognition has been heightened by the incorporation into moral reflection of the insights of sociology regarding the influence of societal structures, for good or ill, on the individual person.

Catholic attention to structural injustice was also focused in the 1960s by the discussion and statements of the World Council of Churches. Its 1966 Conference on Church and Society, meeting in Geneva, for example, grappled with the contemporary "theology of revolution." Proponents of the theology of revolution argued that the oppression of persons and their dignity within the context of unjust structures and systems can be understood as a form of violence. Revolution, even violent revolution, may be seen not only as a response to the violence of oppression and an effort to overturn unjust structures but even a concrete demand of the Christian's effort to serve humanity. Such discussions served to focus the attention of the churches on structural evils—even while many repudiated the advocacy of violent revolution.[18]

Peter Henriot has offered a brief sketch of the evolution of the notion of social sin in the church's social teaching, devoting particular attention to the statement of the 1971 Synod of Bishops, *Justice in the World*.[19] The relationship of personal sin and social structures is explicitly noted in *Gaudium et spes* (#25) of Vatican II:

> To be sure the disturbances which so frequently occur in the social order result in part from the natural tensions of economic, political, and social forms. But at a deeper level they flow from man's pride and selfishness, which contaminate even the social sphere. When the structure of affairs is flawed by the consequences of sin, man, already born with a bent toward evil, finds there new inducements to sin, which cannot be overcome without strenuous efforts and the assistance of grace.[20]

The relationship of injustice to structures was a major focus of the statements of the Latin American bishops in their meeting at Medellín, Colombia, in 1968. The bishops insisted on the need for "liberation" from oppressive structures, a theme already being discussed by the emerging Latin American theology of liberation. Attention to the social and structural dimensions of sin was continued when the Latin American bishops met at Puebla, Mexico, in 1979.[21]

The recognition of sin as a social phenomenon in official church documents can be further noted in several sections of the synodal statement *Justice in the World*. The bishops are concerned for "those who suffer violence and are oppressed by unjust systems and structures (#5)."[22] In discussing the need for education for justice, they remark: "But education demands a renewal of heart, a renewal based on the recognition of sin in its individual and social manifestations (#51)."[23] The liturgy has an important role in furthering such education: "The practice of penance should emphasize the social dimensions of sin and of the sacrament (#58)."[24]

Pope John Paul II's 1984 apostolic exhortation, *Reconciliation and Penance*, offers a brief but significant discussion of social sin. Although he expresses concern about certain ways in which the term "social sin" can be understood, the pope clearly intends to present an understanding of sin which includes its social dimension.[25] The pope reaffirms his discussions of "the structures of sin" in his recent social encyclical, *On Social Concerns*, applying it more directly to social, economic, and political problems.[26]

Contemporary European political theology developed in part as a reaction to and rejection of privatized views of Christianity, including privatized notions of sin.[27] Further, the development of liberation theologies has, in particular, advanced the recognition that sin and its effects become embodied in structures, social relationships, and even in attitudes and in worldviews. Especially as Latin American theologians have incorporated elements of Marxist thought, they have placed great emphasis on "praxis" as that activity aimed at transforming reality and all social, economic, and political relationships.[28] Christian activity in the world is therefore aimed necessarily at overturning structural injustices. Furthermore, "liberation," as the goal of divine and human activity in history, is understood to include both the transcendent elements connoted by the term "salvation" and the intramundane elements of political and socio-economic transformation.[29] Sin, from this perspective, is more immediately seen in its social and structural dimensions.

The emerging feminist theology has also emphasized the social nature of sin, especially patriarchal sexism as a root expression of sin. Sin involves a distorted relationality, a violation of mutuality and equality which is embodied and perpetuated in social structures and ideologies which oppress women. Feminist theology, therefore, like Latin American liberation theology, focuses attention on sin rooted in social, economic, political, cultural, and religious/ecclesiastical, structures. Feminist theologians, however, even more than other liberation theologians, emphasize the symbolic, mythic, and linguistic structures which perpetuate injustice.[30]

An appreciation of the social aspects of sin took the form of an explicit theology of "social sin" in the late 1960s and early 1970s. A number of important articles appeared during that time attempting to define and establish the foundations for an understanding of sin as embodied in society and in structures.[31] The term "social sin" and the recognition of the reality has become widely accepted in Roman Catholic theological circles and appeared, with some cautions, even in official magisterial documents. Quite significantly in terms of widespread acceptance of the concept of social sin is its discussion (with examples) in the National Catechetical Directory published in 1979 by the United States Catholic Conference and approved by the U.S. bishops and by the Congregation for the Clergy. Teaching about social sin is thus set forth as official policy for catechesis of all age groups.[32]

And yet, despite the widespread, renewed recognition of sin as a social reality, very few major, systematic studies have appeared since the mid-1970s.[33] Peter Henriot suggests four reasons that a notion of "social sin" continues to be neglected: (1) moral theology has not entirely overcome its orientation toward acts rather than toward actors; (2) the traditional doctrine of "inculpable ignorance" has made it difficult to conceive of any personal responsibility for sin's social aspects; (3) the influence of existentialism and personalism has led to an excessive emphasis on the individual person; and (4) the blurring of the distinction between "legal" and "moral" leads people to believe that if they act according to the law they are therefore acting morally.[34] That sin has *both* personal *and* social dimensions is accepted virtually without dissent in Roman Catholic theology. How precisely the social aspects of sin are to be understood within the context of the wider theology of sin, however, has not yet been systematically and comprehensively addressed.

### How Radical a Reinterpretation?

To what degree do current discussions of social sin represent a reinterpretation of traditional understandings of sin—"traditional" at least in the sense of the last several hundred years? In large measure, the answer to this question seems to depend on how one understands the reality of social sin itself, particularly in its relationship to personal sin. There are, it seems, at least four broad possible positions on the relationship between social and personal sin, each of which builds on and/or reinterprets to some degree the "traditional" theology of sin. These four positions are: (1) social sin represents the social *effects* of individual personal sin; (2) social sin is the *embodiment* of personal sin and injustice in social structures; (3) social sin and personal sin are co-essential components of a comprehensive view of sin; and (4) social sin is the primary meaning of sin of which individual, personal sin is the manifestation. The present section will examine briefly each of these positions, devoting particular attention to the middle two positions.

*The Social Effects of Personal Sin*

That personal sin has social effects is a traditional claim of Christian, and certainly of Roman Catholic, theology.[35] Clearly there are certain sins which cause direct harm to others, such as murder, theft, and assault. Even the most private and individual acts, however, can be said to have social effects. The person in sin is not an effective channel of grace nor a good example for others. His or her separation from God affects others, certainly within the Christian community. Even "private" sins (for example, avaricious thoughts) may eventually become manifest in actions and attitudes which can impact on the attitudes and perspectives of others. It is precisely this recognition of the social effects of personal sin which has been at the foundation of the Roman Catholic understanding of the need for sacramental confession. The Christian's sin, even committed in private, has deleterious effects on others and is thus confessed to the church's official minister.

To recognize that personal sin has social effects suggests the most immediate connection between personal and social sin, and it represents the most narrow possible acceptance of the social reality of sin. Personal and individual sin remains the focus of attention, and responsibility is clearly imputable to individual persons. In this position, there is no explicit reference to sin as in any way independent of individual human agency. Norbert Rigali, like many theologians who discuss social sin, has argued that viewing social sin as a mere aggregate of personal sin is inadequate in expressing the real, though mysterious, human solidarity in sin.[36]

*Social Sin as the Embodiment of Personal Sin*

Beyond the recognition that personal sin has social effects is the further acknowledgement that personal sin may become "embodied" in societal structures and institutions.

Sin once committed becomes independent of the individual agent. Its evil effects continue in history through embodiment in patterns of behavior and relationship and in prevailing attitudes and worldviews. Once embodied in society and its various structures, sin takes on a relatively independent existence, influencing others to sin and inflicting continuing injustice on persons.

In this perspective, "social sin" as the embodiment of personal sin remains basically an *effect* of personal sin. Personal sin remains the prime analogue. Social sin, like venial sin and original sin, is, in the terms inherited from St. Thomas, "sin by analogy." All sin must be understood from the perspective of mortal sin, that is, sin committed by a human agent with knowledge and freedom. Since human agency is required for sin, it is clear that institutions and groups cannot sin, strictly speaking.

This perspective on the relationship between personal and social sin is clearly in line with the traditional scholastic categories in which Roman Catholic theology has discussed the reality of sin. The apostolic exhortation *Reconciliation and Penance* of Pope John Paul II, in recognizing that sin becomes embodied in structures, clearly states that "social sin," however, must always be understood as "sin by analogy."[37] The pope's encyclical letter, *On Social Concerns*, recently reiterates that the ultimate root of "structures of sin" is personal sin—that is, "the *concrete acts* of individuals who introduce these structures, consolidate them and make them difficult to remove."[38] Bernard Häring, though a strong proponent of an understanding of sin as both personal and social, seems ultimately to be aligned with this perspective.[39]

## Social and Personal Sin as Co-Essential

Other contemporary theologians in reflecting on the social reality of sin, however, seem to place greater emphasis on the necessity for any adequate understanding of sin to account at one and the same time for both its personal and social dimensions.[40] For these theologians *both* the personal dimension of sin *and* its social dimensions can be understood only in relation to one another. On the one hand, sin is experienced as fated, external, necessary, universal, inherited, social, bearing down upon the individual, as an illness, as a seductive force; but, on the other hand, it is experienced as personal, individual, free, chosen, a cause for responsibility and blame. The story of Adam and Eve itself demonstrates that sin involves choice and at the same time flows from external pressure on the individual (symbolized both by the snake and by the interaction between Adam and Eve).[41] The recognition of both dimensions of sin is implicit in Pauline discussions of "the reign of sin" and the Johannine discussions of "the world." Human persons are "sin's captives as well as its authors, its victims as well as its agents."[42] Patrick Kerans says of his attempt to develop a theology of "sinful social structures":

> We have been trying to work away from a simplistic notion of 'full knowledge' and 'full consent' required in order to speak of sin. At the dark moment of decision it seems that it is the allurement and power of evil which is paramount; it is only later, in the moment of conversion, that a person recognizes, to his bitter remorse, that he was personally, freely responsible.[43]

The theology of sin which results from discussions of "social sin" seems, therefore, to be a more fundamental reinterpretation of what sin itself means. In a sense, the tradition has recognized the two related experiences of sin as somehow both external and internal, but has used the word "sin" properly of its personal, internal dimension and only analogously of its social, external dimension. Many of those who advocate a theology of social sin, however, propose that the term "sin" must be used properly of both experiences. From this perspective on sin, each human agent would still have to accept responsibility for sin, but he or she would also be aware of "all for which he was not responsible, but which weighs in on him, enticing him, frightening him, almost forcing him to sin."[44] Objecting to Pope John Paul II's statement that social sin is "sin by analogy," Thomas Schindler argues that "personal sin" is no less an analogical concept than the concept of "social sin." This is necessarily so because no concept can totally express the mysterious reality of sin.[45]

Rosemary Ruether argues that sin always has both a personal and systemic side. It is never simply "individual" in the sense of being private or nonrelational. Sin exists "precisely in the distortion of relationality, including relation to oneself." These relational distortions are perpetuated in social structures and ideologies. Even sins which seem primarily a personal violation of self or of only one other individual take place in a systemic, historical, and social context.[46] This "dynamic interconnection" between the personal and social dimensions of sin cannot be lost without a serious distortion of the understanding of sin.[47]

For Kerans, there is an "historical need" for a notion of social sin.[48] The present situation of society cannot be adequately reflected upon without such a notion. The concept of social sin is precisely an understanding of contemporary social situations of oppression and injustice in light of Christian symbols. To approach these situations without an adequate contemporary notion of sin and forgiveness is to render the Christian message meaningless to those who suffer oppression from these situations. In order for Christians to preach the forgiveness which challenges and allows change, they must first help society to account for its sinfulness.

Gregory Baum is a strong proponent of a theology of sin which recognizes both its personal and social dimensions. He

urges a "dialectical" understanding of the relationship between personal and social sin. At the same time, however, he
argues that the development of an understanding of social sin
must not ignore personal freedom and responsibility. A theology of social sin, he argues, must always maintain a twofold
analysis, both personal and social. Neglect of the social analysis would "let society off the hook, encourage the privatizing
trend, and draw upon a false understanding of human life."
On the other hand, neglect of personal analysis would entail
underestimating "personal freedom and in this way distort the
image of human life."[49] Pope John Paul II, in criticizing certain notions of social sin, shares the same concern to insure
that the human person's freedom and responsibility be adequately recognized and that any notion of "social guilt" recognize its foundation at some point in true personal sin.[50]

Patrick McCormick suggests that the emphasis on personal freedom and knowledge in the act of sin is a significant
aspect of the experience of sin. Yet, it is much like a photo-
graph or a still life of sin—it captures the act of freely choosing
but it cannot bring into its limited focus the full experience of
sin which includes dynamic and social factors in the "larger
picture."[51] The point is not to deny either that personal sin
involves free choosing nor even that at some level evil structures are built up and sustained by individual choices; rather,
the point is that social sin has in fact taken on a virtually
independent existence in the social world which is then unavoidably part of the individual's experience of sin.

McCormick furthermore suggests six models/metaphors
for understanding the experience of sin.[52] The first three—sin
as stain (defilement), sin as crime, and sin as personal—focus
on sin as personal and at least the latter two focus on sin as an
individual choice for which one bears responsibility. The second three models/metaphors—sin as spiral, sin as sickness,
and sin as addiction—focus more (though not exclusively) on

sin as an external power impinging on the human person. Taken separately, these final three metaphors might suggest that sin as a social and external reality is primary and persons "merely" participate in or cooperate with social sin. McCormick, however, suggests that each metaphor captures an aspect of the mysterious reality of sin; thus, together, they may be taken to represent the co-essential nature of personal and social sin.

It seems to be the case that the difference between understanding social sin as co-essential with personal sin on the one hand and understanding it as an embodiment of personal sin on the other may reflect a nuance of difference based on different starting points. If one begins the discussion of sin from the traditional starting point and with traditional categories of the requirements for human agency, then social sin appears as "sin by analogy." This is the case precisely because sin can be fully imputed only to an agent with intellect and will. If, however, one begins from the *experience* of sin as both freely chosen and yet almost imposed from without, then personal and social sin seem co-essential to any definition of sin.

Despite the divergent starting points and conclusions, in the final analysis proponents of a co-essential understanding of personal and social sin may not be in radical disagreement with the more traditional view of social sin as sin by analogy. Baum, as quoted above, seems unwilling to accept any notion that institutions, lacking moral agency, can truly sin. In a sense, therefore, the practical differences between the two positions may not be as extreme as might initially appear. The traditional Roman Catholic moral anthropology which places great emphasis on reason and will, knowledge and freedom, as prerequisites for true sin remains as a presupposition if not as a starting point. Significant differences remain between those who see personal and social sin as co-essential and those who

understand social sin as "sin by analogy," but these differences should not be exaggerated.[53]

## Social Sin as Primary

It remains as a logical possibility to maintain that social
sin is the primary analogue by which sin is to be understood.
Sin would then be understood to be primarily a social reality
which becomes manifest in personal sin. Thomas Schindler
seems closest to this position.[54] He argues that original, personal, and social sin must all be understood as references to
the one mysterious reality which we call "sin." Original sin
refers to the universality of the human opposition to God's
reign; social sin refers to the social and historical forms that
this opposition takes; and personal sin refers to "the ways in
which we as individuals actively participate in that opposition."[55] Schindler maintains that personal sin must be understood to refer to "our participation in, and thus our responsibility for, original-social sin."[56] Social sin, therefore, is not a
mere consequence of personal sin. Schindler argues that sin
must be understood broadly to include "the conscious *and*
unconscious, the deliberate *and* indeliberate ways by which
we participate in and contribute to original-social sin."[57] At
least on the face of it, Schindler's understanding of sin, personal and "original-social," seems a more explicit and fundamental reinterpretation of what the recent Catholic tradition
has understood by the term "sin."

Positions which would maintain that institutions can sin,
strictly speaking, might also be included in the category of
"social sin as primary." To accept it, without substantial clari-
fications, however, would seem an implicit denial of human
freedom and responsibility for sin. It does not seem that any
of the Catholic proponents of a theology of sin would maintain such a position.

**Conclusion**

Though disagreements exist as to the exact nature and range of a concept of social sin, it is a clear affirmation of the Christian tradition that sin is a social as well as a personal reality. This chapter has attempted to indicate the historical roots of the theology of social sin and some of the factors which have caused its decline and contemporary renewal. Further, we have examined the question of how radically a current theology of social sin reinterprets the traditional understanding of sin itself. This sets the stage for the next chapter which will examine the terms, definitions, and metaphors currently in use to denote sin as a social reality.

# 2. Terms and Definitions

A variety of terms is used to designate the reality of sin as a social phenomenon, each with a slightly different connotation. Often different theologians using the same term or using different terms bring different emphases to a theology of social sin. The present chapter will examine the various terms and definitions used for sin as a social reality and some possible metaphors which may help to grasp the mysterious reality of sin as social more accurately. Closer analyses of the terms and their connotations should further clarify the concept of social sin. The terms themselves should not be understood as mutually exclusive.

## Terms and Definitions

*Sin of the World.* One of the most noted and earliest contemporary discussions of the social reality of sin was offered by Dutch theologian, Piet Schoonenberg, especially in his *Man and Sin.*[1] Tracing the biblical discussions of sin, he noted that sin is discussed as a social phenomenon. Since the sin of the first parents, history itself has been imbued with sin, individual sins forming a collectivity which constitutes the "sin of the world." Men and women enter into, "are situated" in, this sinful world. Here Schoonenberg uses the term "being-situated" in a distinctive personalist philosophical

26

sense to express both the intrinsic and extrinsic reality of the human "situation." "Being-situated" is a constitutive factor of human existence including the person's ability to know and choose authentic values. Thus, "being situated" in the sin of the world influences the human person at his or her core.

More specifically Schoonenberg draws a close connection between this "sin of the world" and "original sin." The theological problems in regard to the doctrine of original sin raised by Schoonenberg need not concern the present discussion. It is at least apparent that if sin is a reality which is personal as well as social and inherited, then both clear connections and careful distinctions among personal, social, and original sin would have to be made. As yet, this does not seem to have been done in any systematic manner. In any case, the term "sin of the world" expresses at least the social manifestation of the inherited disorder called original sin and the historical effects of personal choices in the world.

*Sin-solidarity.* Bernard Häring, who has devoted considerable study to the phenomenon of sin in his works of the last thirty-five years, also discusses the social reality of sin under the designation of the "sin of the world." By the use of this term, he seems to understand the social reality of sin in much the same manner as Schoonenberg, including the personalist understanding of the human person as "situated." More distinctive in regard to Häring, however, is the term "sin-solidarity" by which Häring seems to intend the mysterious unity of all persons in sin, both in the origins of the inclination to sin and in sin's embodiment in the social world.[2]

Human persons, all part of one human family under one creator and parent, are inherently connected in a relationship of solidarity. After the fall, this solidarity itself is unavoidably tainted by sin. As Häring himself says: "From Adam, through original sin and through the greater and greater accumulation of total guilt of individuals and all communities together, a fearful current of corruption, a staggering unholy solidarity continues to act in human history."[3]

Häring carries the discussion of "sin-solidarity" further by noting that human solidarity extends as well to the whole created order. It thus takes on "cosmic dimensions" as other persons and creation itself are affected by human sinfulness. Citing Romans 8:19–23, Häring argues that the whole creation "groans inwardly" as it awaits freedom from the bondage of sinful decay and the fullness of redemption. The cosmic nature of sin is perhaps most explicitly manifest in the damage done to the environment by modern industrial society and in the ecological consequences yet to be passed on to future generations.[4]

The term "sin-solidarity" usefully emphasizes the inherent connection of human persons in sinfulness. It does not seem, however, sufficiently to connote the more concrete embodiment of sin in social relationships and structures. Häring himself does not offer precise distinctions in regard to what he calls "the sin of the world," "sin-solidarity," and original sin. A very brief discussion of their connotations in Häring's work may help to enlighten the relationship of these concepts.

In summary, for Häring, "sin-solidarity" represents the mysterious unity of sinful men and women with one another, with Satan, and with the forces of evil, which spreads to encompass the whole of the created order. It implies an almost enigmatic, spiritual bond, a mysterious and profound inner relationship of corruption. The "sin of the world," on the other hand, seems to represent the more external manifestation of this perverse unity. It is the cumulative effects of the sinful heritage of humankind which has become rooted in the whole environment and which impinges on every human person drawing him or her into the mysterious solidarity of perdition. It would seem accurate, then, to say that "solidarity in sin" is the more inclusive, though more interior reality, while "sin of the world" represents the external manifestation of that reality which continues to influence men and women in the world and in the solidarity they inevitably share.

At times, Häring comes close simply to equating "original sin" with the "sin of the world." This identification may be quite intentional but not entirely accurate to the experiences which the terms seem intended to signify. In *Sin in the Secular Age*, Häring makes use of the scholastic distinction which may explain his understanding of the relation between original sin and the sin of the world: *peccatum originale originans* (how sinfulness began in the world) and *peccatum originale originatum* (the sinfulness present in the world which results from all earlier sins). It would seem that the reality expressed in the Adam and Eve story as well as the origin of sin-solidarity itself is represented by *peccatum originale originans*, while *peccatum originale originatum* expresses the reality represented by "the sin of the world."[5]

*Social Sin.* The term "social sin" is by far the most popular designation for the reality of sin as a social phenomenon. Peter Henriot and Gregory Baum, whose definitions of social sin are discussed in the present section, highlight slightly different aspects of sin as a social phenomenon in their use of the term "social sin."

For Peter Henriot, "social sin" refers to: (1) structures that oppress human beings, violate human dignity, stifle freedom, impose gross inequality; (2) situations that promote and facilitate individual acts of selfishness; and (3) the complicity or silent acquiescence of persons who do not take responsibility for the evil being done.[6] Thus, a welfare system which subtly penalizes or demeans the poor, tax systems that allow individual citizens to preserve their privileges at the expense of the poor, and silent acceptance of international trade and monetary systems which injure third world nations are all examples of social sin at work. Social sin is understood by

Henriot, therefore, to be manifested both internally and externally, as structures and situations and as complicity or acquiescence.

Gregory Baum offers a very helpful distinction between social sin defined in terms of its object (i.e. social sin as the evil acts of individual persons or groups of persons that adversely affect society) and social sin defined in terms of its subject (i.e. the community, a collectivity).[7] Sin defined purely in terms of its object does not situate the sinfulness of the world at a deep enough level since it remains on the level of conscious and deliberate action, the realm of personal sin. Baum proposes that social sin be defined primarily in terms of its subject. Social sin, he argues, resides in groups and in communities.

Further, Baum distinguishes four levels of social sin: First is the level of the injustices and dehumanizing trends built into various institutions—social, political, economic, religious—which embody people's collective life. Second is the level of the cultural and religious symbols, operative in the imagination and fostered by society, that legitimate and reinforce the unjust situations and intensify the harm done to people. These symbolic systems Baum identifies as "ideologies." Third is the level of the false consciousness created by these institutions and ideologies through which people involve themselves collectively in destructive action. The false consciousness convinces them that their actions are in fact good. Conversion, as a recovery from the blindness caused by false consciousness, occurs primarily at this level. Fourth is the level of the collective decisions, generated by the distorted consciousness, which increases the injustices in society and intensifies the power of dehumanizing trends. This is the realm where personal sin most clearly enters into the creation and expansion of social sin. It is clear that for Baum, as for Henriot, social sin is manifested both internally and externally.

By way of example, Baum suggests that world hunger is produced not so much by evil choices by individuals but by the very systems by which foodstuffs are produced and distributed. This represents the first, or systemic, level of the reality of social sin. At the second level are the cultural and religious symbols which operate to legitimate the free market system. This is intimately related to the third level of social sin at which persons within the system are unable to envision the possibility of different systemic arrangements because of the false consciousness created by the system itself and its legitimating symbols. Finally, at the fourth level, individual corporate decisions are made about food distribution for the sake of profit rather than with concern for those who are in dire need.

The official commentary on the National Catechetical Directory notes that the consultation process on the Directory uncovered significant opposition to the term "social sin." Some of its critics argued that it can seem to imply that individuals have no personal responsibility. Some preferred to speak of the "social consequences of sin." The commentary argues, however, that the latter term fails to connote adequately the institutional, structural, and systemic nature of sin. The authors of the Directory finally chose to retain the terms "social sin" (in quotation marks) as a more faithful reflection of the institutional emphases in recent papal pronouncements on social justice.[8]

The term "social sin" may further seem to imply that social institutions themselves may "commit sin." This would be clearly contrary to the traditional Catholic foundation of sin in human freedom and knowledge which cannot be predicated of institutions. As was noted in the previous chapter, Catholic theologians who discuss social sin in general repudiate any notion of collective guilt. Baum, for example, argues that what is proper to social sin is that it is not produced by deliberation and free choice. Social sin must, therefore, be understood to produce evil consequences in the community but no guilt in the ordinary sense.[9]

Thomas Schindler argues that social sin is the "specific, concrete form that original sin takes in a particular culture and a particular generation."[10] Original sin "points to the universality of the opposition to God's Reign" while social sin involves "the social and historical forms that opposition takes."[11] Schindler's understanding of the relationship between social sin and original sin seems close to Schoonenberg's understanding of the relationship between the "sin of the world" and original sin.

*Structural Sin* ("Sinful Social Structures," "Systemic Sin"). Patrick Kerans, rather than discussing "social sin," discusses "sinful social structures." The use of this term highlights some of the elements of the social reality of sin already suggested by Henriot and Baum. Social structures, Kerans argues, can meaningfully be said to be sinful in source and in consequences.[12] A social structure can be sinful in its source as it emerges and develops out of individual and personal decisions which are biased, narrow, and destructive. A structure can be sinful in its consequences when "others confronted with a situation so structured are provoked to react defensively and so to reinforce the destructive characteristics of the situation. Still other people, lacking the power to react defensively, will experience sharp limitations on their effective scope of freedom and hence will experience the structure as offensive to their human dignity."

Similar understandings of structural sin are offered by William Byron, Peter McVerry and Patrick McCormick. Byron, identifying structures as "institutionalized sets of interdependent human relationships," argues that social structures become sinful when "they not only embody our greed but survive as a result of our hard-heartedness and sloth."[13] McVerry identifies sinful structures as "those formal sets of relationships which result in the oppression of groups of people, while enabling other groups of people to benefit from that oppression, even without those benefiting fully knowing or fully consenting to the oppression."[14] McCormick believes that it is meaningful to speak of evil or sinful structures and systems insofar as they represent "the structural establishment and official sanctioning of sinful attitudes and disordered, alienated, and unjust relationships. They are both the full flowering of personal and actual sin as well as the unquenching thirst from which social sin will ever continue to grow."[15]

Liberation theologians in particular emphasize the structural sin involved in the economic relationships which prevail between first and third world nations and between the rich and the poor within third world countries themselves. These theologians argue that the institutions of modern capitalism itself create injustice for poor persons and for poor nations. These structures, built up and maintained by greed, oppress the poor who are powerless to overcome them. These structures operate so pervasively and subtly that the poor themselves can come to accept them as the only possible structuring of society. Liberation theologians, therefore, emphasize the need for "conscientization" by which the poor are awakened to their own suffering and to the possibility of liberation.

On the other hand, Michael Novak has argued recently that since human persons are sinners, all human structures will in some way be "sinful structures." What is needed, therefore, he argues, is not the utopian effort to create sinless structures but rather the effort to create structures which will encourage creativity even while they provide appropriate checks and balances to the destructiveness of human sin. Thus "structures of sin" must yield to "structures of virtue" which will provide incentives for people to serve the common good and which will promote personal and social virtue. These structures of virtue will better enable the poor to participate in the goods of society. Such a system, Novak argues, is to be found, not in any forms of socialism, but precisely in democratic capitalism.[16]

Feminist theologians similarly point to the structural sin of patriarchy by which male dominance is assured by structures which oppress women.[17] Once again, these sinful structures are built up and maintained by selfish desires for dominance, and they operate so pervasively and subtly that both men and women can remain relatively blind to the oppression they cause and to the possibility for transformation. Patriarchal structures include not only external social, economic, and political relationships but also the more subtle attitudes and worldviews legitimated by the cultural and religious symbols of patriarchy and learned in the socialization process by both males and females. The first draft of the U.S. bishops' pastoral letter on women's concerns discusses the sin of sexism precisely as a structural evil.[18]

Elements of this patriarchal ideology include sexist language and symbols, the nonverbal language of dress and body signals, laws, and customs. Recently feminist theologians have devoted particular attention to patriarchal structures evident in religious myths (for example, the myth of female evil in the Christian story of Eve and the Greek myth of Pandora)[19] and in scripture and its interpretation.[20] The emphasis on symbols and myths seems to correspond with what Baum identifies as the "second level" on which social sin operates.

The term "structural sin" places great emphasis on the embodiment of sin in structures and systems. Its use may seem to connote an almost exclusive emphasis on the external embodiment of sin, though it may be immediately noted that the discussion of myths and symbols as "internal structures" demonstrates that to speak of "structures" is not necessarily exclusively extrinsic. The use of the term "structures," however, much like Schoonenberg's term "being-situated," is meant to indicate both the external as well as the internal influences of sin as a social reality. Structures operate not only outside individual persons but also within them.[21]

*Comment.* Each of the various terms used to designate the social reality of sin provides a slightly different perspective on sin as a social phenomenon. All of them, however, to varying degrees emphasize the fact that sin, even as social, exercises its influence on persons both externally and internally. In the next chapter, we will examine how this influence functions. In the discussions which follow, the text will use "social sin" as the term with the broadest connotation, though it will be used virtually interchangeably with the terms "sinful social structures" or "structural sin."

## Metaphors for Social Sin

Patrick Kerans has argued that the development of a theology of social sin requires a "recapitulating metaphor" of social sin. The experience and reality of sin, he argues, cannot be reduced to a concept or a definition. Rather, social sin, like sin in general, may best be rendered by a metaphor or a set of interrelated metaphors.[22] Patrick McCormick's study of sin, *Sin as Addiction*, is devoted to the critical examination of a number of different models and metaphors for sin. None of the metaphors is right or wrong; rather each offers a different perspective from which to grasp the reality of social sin.

*Slave-will.* First, Kerans offers the metaphor first used by Luther but developed by Paul Ricoeur—"slave-will."[23] This metaphor points to the experience of the "opaque mystery" of the tension between freedom and the power of evil. As sinners reflect back on their sin, they recognize that they were in a situation which was not entirely neutral. Before they made their decision, they experienced the evil in some ways as external, as powerful, and as fascinating. They were, in a sense, "captivated" by temptation; and the captivation became a captivity when it became freely willed. Thus, the metaphor of "slave-will" points to the paradoxical experience of a freedom freely given over to captivity, a captivity to an evil presented at least partially from outside the person. Thus sin arises from a choice but a choice which was influenced by the captivation with an external "power." Kerans himself also refers, in a similar way, to persons being "freely in bondage."[24]

*Collaboration.* Dorothee Soelle discusses sin as "collaboration," suggesting that people freely cooperate with the power of sin in the world around them.[25] They are collaborators with "a structurally founded, usually anonymous injustice." An authentic understanding of sin becomes supplanted by a "feeling of powerlessness" in the face of evil which leads to passivity in the face of injustice. It is precisely the social sciences, especially sociology, which help to identify the manner in which people unconsciously cooperate with anonymous injustices and which suggest paths for overcoming their influence.

*Knowingly Ignorant.* Kerans offers the metaphor of "knowingly ignorant," language inspired by the work of Bernard Lonergan.[26] Lonergan uses the word "scotosis" to refer to the unconscious process of blocking understanding; further, he analyzes the manner in which persons deliberately choose to abandon certain lines of inquiry and pursue others or adopt certain perspectives and exclude others. After examining the usefulness of the metaphor of "knowing ignorance," Kerans offers an analysis of economic equality as an example of the manner in which social sin works, how the affluent allow themselves to be unaware of the plight of the poor and to "cherish the illusions" which keep them in their own privileged position.[27] Bernard Häring seems to be pointing to the same reality in referring to the "blindness" which sin may entail. Further, one of the scriptural terms which Häring uses to identify sin in general is *"skotos"* (darkness).[28]

*The Demonic.* Gregory Baum suggests that the category of the "demonic" points to the evil at work in the world which cannot be simply reduced to individual human malice.[29] The "demonic" points to the manner in which the evil that begins with human choices escapes immediate personal control. The evil establishes itself in human history and is perpetuated by forces which seem largely outside the control of any particular person or even whole groups of people. "Every institution, the best of them, is affected by pathological trends that multiply evil. The person caught in these processes faces an inhuman power, impersonal, relentless, devouring, similar to some of the biblical descriptions of the demonic."[30] Baum points in particular to the manner in which the "demonic" is present in the political order and in the power of its institutions. Anyone who fails to take into account the power of these "demonic" elements will be overly optimistic concerning the possibility of change and the means to attain it.

Bernard Häring seems to be making the same point when he discusses the role of Satan and the devils in the "great eschatological battle" which is taking place in the environment.[31] Pope John Paul II also seems to be alluding to the same reality when he discusses "the mystery of sin":

> Clearly, sin is a product of man's freedom. But deep within its human reality there are factors at work which place it beyond the merely human, in the border-area where man's conscience, will and sensitivity are in contact with the dark forces which, according to St. Paul, are active in the world almost to the point of ruling it.[32]

*Other Biblical Metaphors.* Various biblical metaphors are also used to designate social sin. The figure of the serpent in the Adam and Eve story is a witness to the external nature of sin which precedes personal choosing, just as the interaction between the man and the woman witnesses the interplay between persons in the moment of choice. In the New Testament, the letter to the Romans (5–8) is concerned with the "reign of sin," implying the power of sin in the world external in a sense to personal choosing. Both the Pauline and especially Johannine use of the term "the world" often carry the pejorative sense of the created order hostile to God and to Christ (e.g. 1 Jn 5:19). The "world," so understood, exercises a deleterious influence on persons which disciples of Jesus must resist (e.g. Jn 15:19; 1 Jn 2:15). Pauline literature also contains similar metaphors such as references to "principalities and powers" which further indicate sin as a social reality (e.g. 1 Cor 2:8; Eph 6:12).[33]

*Virus, Disease, Sickness, Contagion.* Patrick McCormick suggests a series of metaphors to express the reality of sin which is experienced as both personal and social.[34] Of special relevance to the theology of social sin are a number of metaphors which are centered on the experience of illness. Sin is like a virus or a cancer which grows within the sinner and which spreads from one individual to another, from one generation to another. Sin, like disease, if untreated leads inexorably to death. This series of metaphors highlights the "pathological" nature of sin and its tendency to be "contagious" in the social world. Mixing his metaphors a bit, McCormick goes on to suggest that sin becomes a "spiral" in which the sin of individuals continues to feed and is fed by the contagion of sin from without.

*Addiction.* As the title of McCormick's book indicates— *Sin as Addiction*—a primary metaphor by which he wishes to understand sin is "addiction."[35] In relation to the individual person, the image of addiction connotes the habitual nature of sin and the relative diminution of freedom which characterizes our experience of sin—this in contrast to an over-emphasis on sin as an act. Recognizing that the metaphor of addiction can imply a denial or at least a serious mitigation of human freedom and responsibility, McCormick discusses the interpersonal and even societal levels at which addiction can operate. He notes, for example, the manner in which whole family systems cooperate in an addictive process even over several generations. The metaphorical use of "addiction" highlights the experience of sin as an external power which is precisely an essential element of the experience of sin as social.

*Woundedness and Healing.* James Hug suggests the need to move away from the rhetoric of sin and guilt and instead to develop metaphors of woundedness and healing.[36] "Social sin" refers to the "woundedness" of a community "carried in its institutions, policies, and procedures as well as in the hearts of its people." In response to the social reality of sin, societal critics call for change and even revolution, but this approach only evokes passive resistance or active rebellion by men and women of good intentions who are threatened by this denunciation. It is therefore more fruitful, says Hug, to speak of the need for a therapeutic healing of society. Bernard Häring develops the notion of a therapeutic approach to dealing with societal problems without resorting to violence.[37] Correlative to his use of the metaphors of disease and addiction for sin, McCormick argues for metaphors of "healing" and "recovery" as the necessary response to sin.[38]

*Comment.* As Kerans has suggested in offering possibilities for a "recapitulating metaphor" for social sin, no one metaphor fully captures the reality of sin. Yet, each captures some aspect of the experience of social sin. These metaphors in general render the mysterious and even paradoxical nature of sin in a manner which cannot be expressed in concepts and definitions.

**Conclusion**

The present chapter has attempted to examine terms and metaphors currently in use to denote the social reality of sin. Each brings to a theology of social sin a slightly different connotation which together seem to enhance a broad understanding of social sin. The next chapter will look more narrowly at the theological and, more especially, the sociological foundations for a theology of social sin.

# 3. A Sociological-Theological Perspective

Peter Henriot has argued that the framework for understanding social sin "consists of a *sociological* emphasis on the reality of social structures and a *theological* interpretation of the meaning of sin."[1] Sociology provides the scientific means by which to analyze the manner in which injustice can become embodied in social structures and continue to influence individual persons. Theology provides the interpretive framework which allows us to understand human injustice within the broader perspective of humankind's relationship with God—and more specifically, as the violation of that relationship, which is sin. Thus, as Henriot indicates, understanding social sin and how it works requires the insights provided by both sociology (together with other social sciences) and theology.[2]

A frequently cited work in the various discussions of social sin is the 1966 work of Peter A. Berger and Thomas Luckmann, *The Social Construction of Reality*.[3] Berger and Luckmann, within the context of a general sociological perspective, are particularly concerned with the sociology of knowledge, that is, the manner in which knowledge is affected by social forces. With differing emphases and vocabulary, theologians reflecting on the reality of social sin use such sociological insights to analyze the working of social sin. After a brief note on theological anthropology, the present chapter will explicate some of the major sociological concepts and terminology which have been brought to bear in the study of social sin.

## A Note on Theological Anthropology

Before discussing the sociological analyses in regard to social sin, a few words should be offered concerning a basic presupposition of Roman Catholic theological anthropology: the human person is inherently social. This presupposition concerning human nature is an important foundation for Roman Catholic social ethics and official Catholic social teaching. The human person, uniquely personal and individual, develops fully only within the context of community. Human persons are created with an inherent relationship with one another, for good or ill. Human sin—even when apparently private and individual—therefore inevitably pervades human relationships after the fall, though it must be added immediately, on the other hand, that grace too pervades these relationships, bringing persons together in anticipation of a salvation which will be both personal and social. Individual human persons are saved in community from sin which is both individual and social.

The fact that human existence, uniquely personal and social, is inextricably bound up in social, economic, political, and cultural structures is at least implicit in the social encyclicals since Leo XIII's *Rerum novarum* in 1891. Justice can be attained and the rights of the poor and of workers protected only through attention to the structural obstacles to change. The recognition of the multiplicity and complexity of these structures in the contemporary world increases in the more recent encyclicals. Of particular note is John XXIII's discussion of "the complexity of social structure" and the increase of social relationships ("socialization") in his encyclical *Mater et magistra* in 1961 (#59–67).[4]

The relation of the human person to other persons extends not only to persons alive in the present historical moment. The human person is not only social but historical—related to those who have gone before and to those who will follow after. As Bernard Häring argues, the human person constitutes history and is constituted by history.[5] Thus, as we shall see, sin becomes embodied in social structures that continue in history; and sin thus embodied is passed on—inherited—from one generation to the next.

### The Sociological Grounds of Social Sin

Sociology studies groups and human persons in groups. Thus, while it is directly concerned with studying social interactions between and among persons, sociology in a sense presupposes that persons are intimately interrelated with their social context. Because of sociology's focus of study, it is clearly the most useful social science to study the embodiment of sin in social institutions and its subsequent effect on human persons within this social context. According to Berger and Luckmann, the human person exists in a dialectical relationship with the social world within which he or she lives. Individual and society are in constant interaction, in a reciprocal relationship which Berger and Luckmann characterize in the following summary: "Society is a human product. Society is an objective reality. Man is a social product."[6] Any attempt to understand the individual and his or her social world must take into account each of the three statements in this summary.

Summarizing the work of Berger and Luckmann, Peter Henriot discusses the three "moments" in the dialectical process of the genesis and maintenance of social institutions and structures. The first "moment" in this process is "externalization." ("Society is a human product.") This is the manner in which human persons superimpose order on the environment in order to make it more meaningful and useful. The second "moment" is "objectivation." ("Society is an objective reality.") This is the process by which the product of human externalization is experienced as an autonomous reality confronting the individual as an external and coercive fact. The final "moment" in this process of "making society" is "internalization" which is the process by which structured reality is passed from generation to generation in the course of socialization.[7] ("Man is a social product.") The discussion below will further explicate these three moments in the dialectical relationship of person and society under the subheadings: "Persons Make Society" (incorporating externalization and objectivation) and "Society Makes Persons" (internalization).

## Persons Make Society

Sociology reveals the degree to which all social structures and institutions are built up over time by human decision, action, and cooperation. Enduring social structures, at the earliest stage of formation, are grounded in some sort of voluntary action or relationship. These structures or institutions essentially involve value-relationships; that is, they reflect the values of those who construct them. As Henriot points out, a political structure such as a democratically elected representative assembly, an educational structure such as compulsory education for children, and familial structures such as patriarchy or matriarchy embody the meanings and values of those who construct them.[8] The process of building up these structures is "externalization."

These actions or value-relationships then become pat-

terned and thus no longer involve conscious approval or decision-making. As the structure continues over time—we
might say "takes on a history"—it becomes relatively independent of any choosing, though its continuance does depend
on the continuing cooperation (albeit largely unconscious) of
human agents within the established patterns. This is called
"objectivation." It may thus be said that persons make society
and its structures—if it is kept in mind that the vast majority
of the human action required to build up these structures does
not involve any conscious choice in creating or continuing
society and its constituent structures.

Objectivation may be carried as far as "reification"—that
is, the objectified products of human activity may be viewed
as if they were something other than human products.[9] Rather
than understanding certain social structures and institutions
as the result of human action, people can come to understand
them as a fact of nature or the result of a cosmic law or a
manifestation of the divine will. Reification demonstrates that
human persons are capable of forgetting their own role in the
construction of the world around them. Once social structures
are understood as dependent on some factor outside of
human action, they become virtually impervious to change.

Clarification of Terms

Despite some diversity in the use of terms to describe
objectified social realities, certain terms are used with some
consistency by theologians reflecting on social sin. Often,
however, such terms are used without careful definitions and
appropriate distinctions. For example, terms such as "structural sin," and "systemic sin" can be taken, in general, to be
virtually synonymous, and yet they may indicate different
nuances or levels of meaning depending on how one understands "structures" and "systems." It seems useful therefore
to offer some definitions for the most frequently used terms
such as "structures," "institutions," and "systems." As will be

noted, when used according to more strictly sociological usage, these terms often connote differing "levels" of social reality. Less frequently occurring (and less precise) terms also merit some attention: "environment," "situation," and "circumstances."

*Structure.* A social structure is an ordered pattern of relations that is established and becomes routine. Structures involve policies and institutions that make up the patterns of societal organization as well as the worldviews, perspectives, and value systems by which we interpret our experiences so as to bring coherence and meaning into our lives. Structures, therefore, are both external and internal to the individual person. These two types of structure are interrelated in any society. In order to bring about a lasting reform of external structures, it is often necessary to bring about a change in the internal structures.

Joe Holland and Peter Henriot argue that the effort to address any social problem will require understanding its complex historical and structural roots.[10] In particular, they are concerned with economic, political, and cultural structures. Economic structures, such as business and commercial institutions, "shape the basic patterns of production, distribution, exchange and consumption within a society." Political structures, "the institutional concentrations of power within a community," involve both the formal institutions of government and the less formal focus of power in various other societal organizations such as trade unions and lobbies. Cultural structures "serve as the institutional bases for the dreams, myths, and symbols of society." Any effort to change these structures, Holland and Henriot argue, will require understanding not only the structures themselves but also the complex interrelations between and among them.

*Institution.* An institution is a distinctive complex of actions, providing procedures through which human conduct is patterned, e.g. marriage and organized religion. Institutions thus provide typologies for our actions. Institutions control human conduct by setting up predefined patterns of conduct. Other forms of social control, whereby individuals are pressured into conformity with prevailing patterns of behavior, merely reinforce the process of institutionalization. Institutions subtly suggest that the patterns they offer are the only patterns available so that other ways of organizing human action can seem only nonsensical or chaotic. Thus, the western male would generally consider the possibility of the institution of marriage organized along the pattern of polyandry unacceptable if not nonsensical.

*System.* A system is a complex of social structures and institutions. Thus we may speak of civil authority systems, systems of exchange, and persuasion systems.

William Byron, S.J., has drawn a more careful distinction between "structures" in relation to "systems":

> I understand social structures to be institutionalized sets of interdependent relationships which influence social behavior and regulate the life chances available to persons at given times and places. The words 'system' and 'structure' are often used interchangeably. I tend, however, to favor the use of system as the more comprehensive and general term. Within a given system, a variety of structures (institutionalized arrangements which affect behavior) are found.[11]

For example, says Byron, there is a criminal justice system that includes the structure of prison life and the appellate court structure; there is a capitalist economic system within which a wage structure operates. In this context, one can seek to transform either systems or structures, though analysis and action in regard to particular structures within a given system may prove the more effective manner in achieving reform.[12]

*Environment, Situation and Circumstances.* Less precise terms (at least from a sociological perspective) are also used to signify the influence of social factors on the individual person.

Bernard Häring has consistently used sociological insights in the process of developing his moral theological discussions, though frequently without engaging in the more precise terminology used by sociologists. Häring draws the terms "environment" (*Umwelt*) and "milieu" from his social scientific studies in order to describe the social factors which surround and influence the development and behavior of the human person. Both environment and milieu are a frequent topic of discussion in his works.[13] Häring seems to use the two terms almost interchangeably, and he does not often define them in a very precise manner. Environment, says Häring, is constituted by the people with whom one comes into direct or indirect contact; but it includes much more: "our cultural heritage, the world in which we live, civilized nature, the conditions of economic and professional life with its organizations and groups, the complex reality of the political life and legislation, of off-time entertainment, particularly however of public opinion which approaches us through thousands of channels."[14] Most broadly, Häring means by "environment" the "spirit of the community . . . everything that helps to shape the world around us and our relationships."[15]

Häring's understanding of "environment" seems very close to Piet Schoonenberg's personalistic understanding of "situation" and liberty as "situated."[16] Schoonenberg defines "situation" as "the totality of the circumstances in which somebody or something stands at a certain moment, the totality of circumstances prevailing in a certain domain." "Being situated" is both a sociological category and one drawn from personalist philosophy which affirms that the situation in which the human person finds himself or herself is not entirely exterior or extrinsic to the human person but rather a constitutive factor in human existence.

Patrick Kerans distinguishes between "circumstances" and "situation."[17] By "circumstances," Kerans understands "all those factors which are 'not me' and over which the person has no control, but which impinge on him." "Situation," on the other hand, connotes interaction by a subject. The situation includes "those factors in a person's circumstances with which he is prepared to deal, of which he is conscious, concerning which he is deciding." If it were possible for human persons to be perfectly objective and omniscient, then their situations would be virtually equivalent to their circumstances. But because human knowledge is limited and because every person is inevitably biased, "each situation is never more than a part of circumstances; and usually a distortion."

According to Kerans, it is in the context of the distinction between situation and circumstance that any individual's freedom and knowledge—and even the framework by which individual persons and groups of persons make sense of reality—must be understood. It is the human ability to bring structure to the many and varied circumstances exterior to self which allows persons to make sense of the world around them. People require the structuring of situations to protect themselves from "the ultimate terror of meaninglessness," the "nightmare of chaos."

## *Society Makes Persons*[18]

Though it may correctly be said that persons make society, it has already been noted that enduring societal structures become relatively independent of human choice. These structures "take on a history" of their own. People are born into societal structures which pre-exist them, which continue without their conscious choosing (and largely without their awareness) and which will perdure long after their demise. So independent do such structures become that they become accepted as the manner in which certain actions *must* be carried out or in which certain relationships *must* take shape; that is, these structures become part of people's views of reality. To suggest that a structure be uprooted becomes tantamount to suggesting the introduction of chaos.

In large measure persons learn their attitudes, values and views of reality from the societal structures in which they are born. What has become objectified becomes internalized— that is, as a child is socialized through the process of informal and formal education and training, he or she internalizes the value-relationships which are the foundation for the structures and institutions of society. If the structures of the society into which one is born enshrine certain values, then one is likely to be aware of and accept these values. If, on the other hand, one's society does not enshrine particular values, then one will be relatively blind to these values—unable to perceive them as worthy of choice. Furthermore, if society holds that certain disvalues are in fact to be valued, then the persons who make up that society are most likely to accept the disvalues as values. For example, feminist theologians argue that it is precisely the socialization of males and females into patriarchal language and value systems that perpetuates these structures.[19]

Bernard Häring in particular emphasizes the importance of society as a teacher of value. The ability to apprehend value is crucial to moral formation since conscience itself is formed in relationship to the social context in which the moral agent finds himself or herself. Thus, as Häring notes, individuals can be "blind" to values precisely because society has failed to embody or enshrine these values.[20] More specifically, Bernard Häring identifies three types of possible value-blindness: (1)

all-pervasive blindness to value, (2) partial blindness to value, and (3) blindness in the concrete application of a type of value. Each type of value-blindness is dependent largely on societal influences on individuals and groups.

All-pervasive blindness to value, says Häring, is found in varying degrees in those who have made a wrong "fundamental option" and thus have failed to find their own true identity. Blind to the basic and absolute value which is God, they are blind also to other values. This blindness is, however, never absolute and final as long as moral freedom and responsibility can be awakened.

Partial blindness to value extends to a particular type of value or even to a group of values. The person is most likely to be blind to higher and more demanding values especially when there is not a continued and profound effort to know and attain them.[21] Partial blindness, however, can coexist with a basic knowledge of good.

In the blindness of the concrete application of a type of value, one recognizes moral value and the types of value in general but fails to discern the application of the value because of his or her own continuing selfishness or pride.

Even those who have attained a sufficient level of insight to question these disordered values may find themselves powerless to overcome the magnitude of reality so perceived within the society. Thus, structures, for better or worse, exercise a great deal of formative influence on persons. This influence is often quite subtle and thus difficult to detect, resist and overcome. One may think, for example, of the perpetuation of values which is carried on through advertising. Feminist theologians point to the subtle influence of exclusive ("sexist") language in subtly but powerfully forming the perceptions of both males and females.

Society can be seen to exercise its influence both externally and internally.

(1) Society Working From Outside

Society and its constituent structures exercise their influence on human persons by a number of means largely external to persons within society (though these means of control are also to some degree internalized). Two of the most important ways in which society influences its members and protects against "deviant," nonconforming behavior are the phenomenon of social control and social stratification.

Perhaps the most basic means of social control—by which society keeps its members in line—is through violence or at least the threat of violence. This threat operates behind any sort of police force. More subtly, social control operates through economic pressure (fear of unemployment for those who "buck" the system); the commonly accepted morality, customs, and manners; and on a more personal level, the fear of ridicule and ostracism which seems to run contrary to a basic human need to be accepted. Closely related and more consciously operative is the reality of "power" which involves the ability to guide and control a group's actions, attitudes, and perspectives. All of these phenomena serve as means of social control—ways in which society and its structures teach values and control behavior.

Another manner by which society influences persons is called "social stratification." Every society consists of levels that relate to each other in terms of subordination and superordination; that is, each society has a system of ranking persons. Liberation theologians, influenced by Marxist analysis, focus especially on the influence of prevailing "class systems" which provide ranking according to economic criteria and by extension according to birth into established economic classes. Feminist theologians similarly emphasize the ranking according to gender which runs across economic classes. It is clear also that class distinctions can also be based in racial, religious, or ethnic background. Further, each society operates with certain social controls which maintain its system of social stratification, and each individual class possesses social controls to control its members within the larger system.

(2) Society Working From Inside

Society further exercises its influence in a more directly interiorized manner (though even the external influences involve a good deal of interiorization). This influence can be viewed from at least three different sociological perspectives: role theory, the sociology of knowledge, and reference group theory.

*Role theory* involves the study of social roles as these are learned from society. This may also be called social differentiation. A role may be understood as a "typified response to a typified expectation." Society provides these typologies, for example, in the expectations which come with the roles of clergy person, of professor, of wife and mother. While various roles have varying degrees of exactness in the range of expectations which they carry, they all direct action and also provide attitudes concerning life in general and how it ought to be lived by the person in that role. In this way external institutions are embodied in persons by means of role expectations.[22]

People are largely born into roles or are subtly guided into assuming them and subsequently receive a good deal of their personal identities from the roles they assume. In this sense it can be said that our identities are "socially bestowed, socially sustained and socially transmitted." These roles are learned as part of the socialization process by which a child learns to be a participant member of society. Since they are learned and remain relatively resistant to change, role expectations play a major part in maintaining societal structures in their current state.

Paralleling the discussion of role theory, Patrick McCormick offers the metaphor of "game" to describe the manner in which people learn to operate in society. Games involve "the habitual patterns of behavior determining the interaction and cooperation among various persons."[23] Each game has rules of conduct and established roles which the various agents/players are expected to accept. Though each person functions freely within the game, the game itself remains the larger context for individual choices.

*The sociology of knowledge* studies knowledge as a social reality. It is concerned with the manner in which knowledge is transmitted in the social context, with knowledge in relation to wider structures and processes of society, with knowledge as the common possession of a group or community rather than with knowledge possessed by discrete individuals. One's view of reality and of one's place in it is largely learned from society. Further, one's values and attitudes—and, to a large degree, even one's self-image and self-perception—are learned. These learned values and attitudes further tend to legitimate and perpetuate the present social situation: explaining, justifying, and sanctifying (that is, the appropriated values and attitudes suggest transcendent approval and the aura of unchanging reality for the present situation).

Christian ethicists, such as Bruce C. Birch and Larry L. Rasmussen, have argued that not only is moral knowledge learned largely from the community but the moral self, including one's moral character, is formed by the social process in the interaction between the self and the social world. A significant part of character formation is the internalization of societal myths, stories, symbols, and traditions. The person's moral vision, dispositions, intentions, conscience, and decision-making are unavoidably situated in the social world. The social world, therefore, not only exists outside the person but, in a sense, exists *within* the person as well.[24]

Beyond its role as a teacher of values, it is society which offers the symbolic apparatus with which we grasp the world and order and interpret our experience. It offers heroes/heroines and myths which serve to enshrine and perpetuate the values held by society. This symbolic apparatus takes on particular form in language by which reality is both assimilated and communicated. Berger and Luckmann discuss the importance of this "symbolic universe" by which persons come to view reality. Feminist theologians in particular emphasize the importance of myths, symbols, and language in perpetuating social sin.

Sociology of knowledge is also concerned with the influence of ideologies by which a certain idea can come to serve a vested interest in society. Frequently an ideology involves a systematic distortion of reality to serve those who benefit from this distortion. Though often operating unconsciously in both those who benefit and those who bear the burden of carrying on the vested interest of a small group, such ideologies legitimate the status quo by leading persons to believe that the present situation is to be accepted as the necessary state of reality. Ideologies may involve such things as sexism, racism, violence, and even "free enterprise." Liberation theologians discuss ideology as a form of blindness which must be overcome through "conscientization" which includes both a "consciousness-raising and critical, transforming action."[25]

Less within the realm directly examined by sociologists of knowledge but related to it is the influence of social structures on the development of human freedom. Freedom as well as knowledge must be acknowledged as a social reality.[26] Not only do persons learn significant values from their social context, but they also learn how to exercise their freedom in choosing to seek values which may be difficult to attain. Where the example of bad choices is prevalent in society, individual persons will be less likely to develop their freedom in such a way as consistently to choose appropriate and significant values.

McCormick suggests that, just as individual free choices exist within the context of the person's habitual dispositions (vices and virtues) which are necessary influences on those choices, so too does the freedom of the individual person exist within the context of the freedom of others and of the community. Individual freedom exists—but it always exists historically as a "situated" freedom. Kerans discusses the reciprocal relationship between freedom influencing environment and environment influencing freedom as the relationship between the social *consequences* of freedom and the social *preconditions* of freedom.[27]

*Reference group theory* is concerned with the reference group as a social source of behavior, opinions, attitudes. A reference group is a collectivity whose opinions, convictions, and courses of action are decisive for the formation of one's own opinions, convictions and decisions. Reference groups provide models with which persons can compare themselves and thus adapt their own outlooks according to the models provided. "Peer pressure" is a particular manifestation of the influence of reference groups on persons within the group.

"Society makes persons" both through exerting external pressure and through learned internal constraints. The human person internalizes the view of reality which society presents to him or her. Society becomes part of us, lives within us.

It should be noted that the recognition of the important role which societal factors play on individual formation is not necessarily a form of determinism. The freedom of individual persons is not entirely restricted by the social structures in which they find themselves. Human persons remain free. On the other hand, sociology and human experience itself remind us that there is no such thing as absolute, sovereign, individual freedom or knowledge.

**Conclusion**

The contemporary theology of social sin builds on the sociological analysis of the relationship between individual persons and the social structures and institutions within which they find themselves. Though human persons, over time, build up and sustain social structures, these structures become relatively independent of human choosing and play a significant role in how persons will understand and react to the world around them. The present chapter has attempted to examine this interaction between person and society. The next chapter will look more explicitly at how social sin operates within the personal/social dialectic.

# 4. Social Sin at Work

Having examined the sociological foundations for a theology of social sin, it may now be possible to examine more directly how social sin operates—that is, how sin becomes embodied in structures which continue the oppression of persons. The present chapter will proceed in the following manner: first, it will briefly examine the relationship between injustice and sin; secondly, the chapter will examine the development of sinful structures and offer a brief example; thirdly, it will discuss the manner in which sin affects moral reflection itself; and finally, the chapter will conclude with a discussion of responsibility for sin.

## From Injustice to Sin

As was noted earlier, a theology of social sin consists of a sociological discussion of the reality of social structures and a theological discussion of the meaning of sin. The previous chapter attempted to present the sociological data. The present chapter attempts to show more explicitly how social sin can be seen to work. It seems necessary first, however, to say a few words on the relationship between injustice and sin. Clearly sin is a theological term—it involves an explicit relationship with God which is not necessarily the case with the term "injustice."

Why are acts of injustice or oppression or marginalization "sin"? Why then are unjust structures also sinful structures? How is it that injustice has reference to God? The relationship of injustice and sin can be looked at from a number of different perspectives. At one level, it may simply be argued that God commands a respect for other persons. Acts committed against other persons violate God's commands, and therefore they involve not only injustice but sin. More fundamental than God's explicit command is the fact that God has created all persons as part of a single human family. There is an inherent solidarity between persons. Inasmuch as God is the one creator and parent of the human family, harm done by one person to another is a violation of the social ordering of persons which God has created—it is therefore sin.

Along the same lines, though more complex, is the relationship between love of God and love of neighbor. As Karl Rahner has shown, reflecting on the two commandments of Jesus and on emphases in the Johannine literature, love of God and neighbor are inseparable.[1] To fail in love of neighbor is to fail in love of God—in this sense, to sin. The unity but distinction between love of God and neighbor allows Richard Gula to distinguish between "transcendent" and "immanent" dimensions of sin.[2] According to Gula, the transcendent dimension expresses the break in one's relation to God. It is the denial of the divine invitation to live with God in love. But since we do not experience our relationship with God apart from our relationship with the world and the persons around us, sin is not only an offense against God but also against God's living images. This is sin's immanent dimension.

Much more could be said of the relationship of injustice and sin (and of love and justice)—particularly of Rahner's discussion—but the concern of this brief discussion has merely been to show that there is an inherent connection between injustice and sin.

**Social Sin at Work**

In the same manner in which it can be said that "persons make society," it is also true to say that persons make social sin. Clearly one unjust situation can simply spawn another without the clear, direct agency of any individual or individuals—in the sense that injustice once established can simply run its course. At least theoretically, however, one should be able to trace the development of a sinful situation to the sinful choices of an individual or group. This is not to deny that sin is inherently both personal and social sin, but merely to say that—inasmuch as social sin is *sin* and inasmuch as structures are built up by human choice and cooperation—sin can (theoretically at least) be traced, however tenuously or remotely, to some event or form of personal choosing. Once the choice is made, its effects then take on a history of their own.

In making the sinful choices, the individual or individuals would most likely (no matter the maliciousness of their intending) never even conceive the direction in which their sin would develop over time. Through the course of history, by mutual consenting and cooperation, the initial sinful choices or actions become patterned—that is, they form structures. The sinful choice and its effects become embodied in external structures and more subtly in the attitudes and perspectives of those involved. Eventually, the accepted pattern comes to be seen as objective reality—both by those who benefit from the established structures and even by those who are oppressed by them. Personal sin (or the sin of persons in groups) has become, over time, embodied in structures, in institutions, and in systems.

Obviously, there would be virtually insurmountable practical difficulties involved in any attempt to identify the precise roots of any particular social sin in historical individuals and groups. To a certain degree, the changing of historical situations can create a situation of injustice where one had not previously existed, even without the apparent choosing of individuals involved in the structures through history. The origins of many social structures are inevitably obscure—though efforts can be made with some success, as feminist efforts to identify the origins of patriarchal structures has shown.[3] Attempting to identify precise roots of structural injustices may serve to provide greater clarity to present injustice and to the necessary steps to overcome the injustice.

At some point, however, regardless of the *origins* of the injustice, the relationship between persons or groups of persons (for example, between men and women) became unjust; and most often the history of this injustice is recognized only in hindsight. Inasmuch as there was an implicit choosing to continue this situation, it may be called "sin." Because of the obscurity of the historical roots of social sin, perhaps the roots of such problems are best grasped in terms of myth—much as the Bible presents the origin of sin and its social manifestations in the mythic stories of Adam and Eve, Cain and Abel, Lamech, the flood.

Persons not only make society—are at the root of all social structures—they also perpetuate it. Similarly, human persons—free moral agents—are not only at the root of social sin (though perhaps remotely), they also perpetuate it. Structures of sin continue to exist because individual people continue to operate freely within them. This is not to say that people freely intend the evil being perpetrated on others; but it is precisely individual people and their choices which perpetuate structures, and when these structures benefit themselves at the expense of others the claim of ignorance must not be introduced too facilely. More must be said of the question of ignorance of social sin and responsibility for it—but it remains important to note that ultimately it is persons who are at the heart of sinful structures and it is persons that perpetuate them.

Persons make society, and sinful persons make social sin. Likewise, just as "society makes persons," so too does sinful society continue injustice and even dispose persons to sin. As the sociological discussion above has indicated, people learn values, attitudes, roles, and even entire perspectives on what constitutes reality from society. The values enshrined by society will in general be accepted as valuable by its members. If certain values are lacking in society, the persons who make up society will be relatively blind to those values. The view of reality which society presents to the individual is relatively resistant to change, and society maintains various means to safeguard its prevailing perspective.

Inasmuch as society is sinful—has embodied sin and injustice—its members will internalize this unjust situation as the very constitution of reality itself. The injustice will be viewed as the only possible manner of constituting society and its structures. Though these structures may be experienced as painful by those who bear the burdens and perhaps as unfortunate by those who carry the benefits, in general neither the oppressed nor the oppressor will perceive the possibility that society can be structured differently. It is precisely for this reason that liberation theology places such great emphasis on the need for "conscientization." And so the situation of injustice continues despite the apparent good will and clear consciences of virtually all the people involved. No single villain or group of villains can be identified. The finger of responsibility cannot be pointed to any particular person or group.

But social sin not only perpetuates injustice, it may also dispose individuals to further personal sin. It does so by clouding their knowledge of values and by crippling their ability freely to choose the good. By clouding their perception of values in general or of significant particular values, social sin disposes persons to choose lesser values in particular situations because the higher values cannot be clearly perceived. Further, even where the values are perceived with some clarity, one's freedom of choice may not be sufficiently strong to act on one's vision. One sees the values present in the situation, but one is unable to choose appropriately because of habitual patterns of acting built on bad example offered by others.

Gregory Baum argues that, as there exists a dialectical relationship between individual and society, so too there exists a dialectical relationship between personal and social sin. Sinful institutions are created, sustained, and furthered by personal sin. These institutions then have profound effects on the people involved with them. Attitudes and perspectives are fostered in people which lead them to further sinful choices. Economic injustices, for example, may encourage greed and materialism in the wealthy just as it can encourage hatred, envy, or despair in the poor.[4]

Piet Schoonenberg argues that the sinful situation in particular influences the person through bad example, through absence of good example (both of which can partially or totally obscure values and norms), and through the absence of grace which is mediated through other persons.[5] James L. O'Connor, S.J., in a brief analysis of Schoonenberg's work, concludes: "Thus solidarity in sin creates a situation of blindness to value and the privation of grace."[6] The privation of grace itself strengthens the natural predisposition to sin already present in fallen human nature.

Bernard Häring discusses the ability of a sinful situation to dispose individuals to personal sin by speaking of "institutionalized temptations."[7] The sinful environment, says Häring, seems to exercise its corrupting influence through the phenomenon of temptation. "In temptation, the sinner's own concupiscence (selfishness) meets with a sinful world around him whose tempting power is the result of all the sins of individuals and groups."[8] In temptation, the sinfulness which has become embodied in the environment finds a "secret ally" within the individual person who exists in a graced-but-sinful order.[9] The tendency to sin inherent within each person encounters in the unhealthy environment those inducements to sin which "match" its own tendencies. *Gaudium et spes* of Vatican II makes a similar point: "When the structure of affairs is flawed by the consequences of sin, man, already born with a bent toward evil, finds there new inducements to sin, which cannot be overcome without strenuous efforts and the assistance of grace."[10]

Temptation arises not simply in the encounter of individual persons in individual situations. As Häring puts it, the sinful environment becomes an accumulation of "institutionalized temptations." The originally individual acts become institutionalized and reinforced through repetition and through embodiment in mutual relationships. The environment becomes polluted in such a way that in its structures and institutions it brings temptations to sin.[11]

**An Example**

Perhaps a brief example of social sin at work may prove useful at this point. Racism in this country has a long and shameful history. A narrative chronicling the sad history of human prejudice based on racial and ethnic differences would probably lead us back to the time following the fall itself. Clearly the first settlers to our country brought with them the racial prejudices which pervaded their homeland at the time —prejudices in particular against black persons and their inherent dignity. The social sin of racism, therefore, clearly predates the establishment of any explicit structures of racism in the United States. In fact, it predates the founding of our nation—though it takes on a particular history here as the structures of the new nation were being formed.

Undoubtedly, some of the founders of our nation were opposed to slavery—seeming to indicate that ignorance of the human dignity and inherent worth of blacks and the evil of the system of slavery could not be claimed by all. In any case, the social sin already present in the attitudes and perspectives of those who settled America were eventually joined with the greed of those who could profit from the structures of slavery —those who sold slaves and those who found that their financial enterprises could profit by the use of slave labor. The institution of slavery and its perpetuation required those who benefited from it effectively to deny the humanity of those enslaved. Prejudice encountered greed and established structures of sin; greed and prejudice perpetuated them.

The intuitive grasping of the dignity and rights of black persons eventually led some to see that the institution of slavery was evil, but the fact that slavery was finally outlawed in the United States did not eliminate the social sin of racism. Racism simply continued in a more subtle form—in the attitudes and prejudices of whites and in the message of white superiority which structures of white dominance sought to teach blacks. The perspectives by which the fundamental dignity and equality of blacks were effectively denied continued to be operative long after slavery was abolished. The social sin of racism manifested itself in such evils as separate facilities and obstacles to adequate education, work, and housing. Though the civil rights movement of the 1960s helped to eliminate many of the most obvious manifestations of racism, attitudes and perspectives which embody and perpetuate racism remain.

The social sin of racism has involved generations of peo-

ple "of good will." They have been largely blind to the evil
perpetuated by the attitudes and the structures which have
oppressed black persons. Racism has been perpetuated inno-
cently in some respects, but it has been perpetuated by subtle
attitudes which—if brought to light—would show themselves
to be an affront to the dignity of other persons. The structures
of sin have been perpetuated too by the subtle complacency of
those who enjoy the benefits which flow from a system which
oppresses others. Prejudice and greed created the social structures of racism; prejudice and greed and complacency have
allowed them to continue.

People raised in a culture in which the sin of racism is
embodied simply take on the sinful attitudes from their parents and those around them. This training need not presup-
pose malicious intent or explicit racism. White children learn
to be part of the sinful structures of racism through hearing
"harmless" racial jokes and epithets. Black children learn
"their place" in society by watching movies and television
shows where all the important plot lines are about white people and all the important roles filled by whites. Children are
subtly educated into the perspectives of racism, and as they
take on adult roles in society they perpetuate the attitudes
which they learned as children. More "people of good will"
are indoctrinated into the social sin of racism.

In their 1979 pastoral letter on racism, "Brothers and
Sisters to Us," the U.S. bishops clearly understand racism to
be an instance of social sin:

> The structures of our society are subtly racist, for these
> structures reflect the values which society upholds. They
> are geared to the success of the majority and the failure of
> the minority; and members of both groups give unwitting
> approval by accepting things as they are. Perhaps no single
> individual is to blame. The sinfulness is often anonymous

but nonetheless real. The sin is social in nature in that each of us, in varying degrees, is responsible. All of us in some measure are accomplices.[12]

## Social Sin and Moral Deliberation

Considering the powerful but largely invisible influence of social sin, the question arises how social sin influences the development and judgments of moral reflection and the existential living out of normative morality itself. In short, how does social sin—embodied in structures and attitudes which have an influence on all people in society—affect the very process of deciding what to do or what kind of person to become? How does social sin affect one's ability to live out the ideals presented by a normative morality?

Josef Fuchs, S.J. addresses this very question in his important article, "The 'Sin of the World' and Normative Morality."[13] In short, Fuchs recognizes that the "sin of the world" may make the overcoming of injustice impossible at the present moment even though people have become aware of it and wish to change it. It may be necessary, he argues, to cooperate for a time with the unjust situation in order to avoid an even greater evil. Though such cooperation under such circumstances will inevitably further the "sin of the world" and its consequences, it is nonetheless not sinful in itself but rather morally good since it involves the choice of "the relatively greater good of a lesser (premoral) evil."[14] This is not to be understood as a passive acceptance of evil but a recognition that—for a time—the evil cannot be overcome.

The "theology of compromise" as developed by Charles E. Curran seems based on the same recognition that the "sin of the world" may prevent the person from attaining a particular good or avoiding a particular evil in the concrete situation.[15] The person may be aware of the injustice of the situation but be relatively unable to overcome it due to the power of the sin operating in both the external and internal structures of the situation. Curran argues that such "compromise" need not be a facile and passive acceptance of evil but is rather a realistic acceptance that moral effort always occurs in a world in which both grace and sin are operative, a world in which the reign of God is only partially realized.

Bernard Häring does not consider the implications of the sin of the world for normative morality with the same careful analysis which characterized the discussions of Curran and especially of Fuchs. His moral theology does, however, seem open to a further development of this theme. The "law of growth" which recognizes the need for a certain gradualism in realizing moral norms and the status of some norms as "goal-commandments" (*Zielgebot*) seem an implicit recognition that the sinfulness present in the situation may justifiably influence the person's moral decision. Because of human sin, persons in concrete situations may only gradually be able to realize the full demands of the relevant norms. While always striving to attain the ideal, persons need to accept the limitations present in the situation and within themselves.

Häring's work further suggests that the traditional categories of cooperation with evil may also offer possibilities for discussing the relationship of the sin of the world and normative deliberation. Moral theological discussions of cooperation offered principles by which one could justifiably cooperate in a situation known to be morally evil. It has been traditional in Catholic moral thought to recognize that it is impossible in a complex and sinful world to avoid all involvement with evil. It was judged acceptable to "cooperate" with some evil, according to distinctions and principles carefully —if variously—defined. Though one could never intend evil ("formal cooperation"), one might be able to offer some material assistance ("material cooperation"). The more immediate and direct the material cooperation, the greater the need for a truly proportionate reason. The question of legitimate cooperation with evil leads to the discussion of attempting to assess responsibility for participation in and perpetuation of social sin.

## Individual Responsibility for Social Sin

Social sin involves the embodiment of sin in unjust structures which exist relatively independent of human agency and conscious choosing. These structures influence persons in such a way that those who suffer the injustice as well as those who benefit from it may be largely blind to injustice at the structural level. Granted that the influence and effects of social sin exist largely outside the realm of individual choosing, can anyone be held responsible for social sin? Does involvement in social sin entangle one in true personal sin? If so, when? How? To what degree? It must be noted at the outset that the purpose of discussing social sin is not to induce paralyzing guilt on sincere people who have previously been blind to their complicity in social sin. Rather, it is to help them to accept the responsibility for changing these structures of sin.

At times, individuals or at least a small group of individuals can be identified as the perpetrators or agents of social injustices; but probably more often, the sinful structures have been built up over such an expanse of time and become so diffuse in a society that no one person or group can be identified as clearly responsible. Obviously, if one were knowingly and willingly to support and enhance an unjust structure of situation, one would somehow be responsible for the injustice which results. In general, however, the phenomenon of social sin involves a certain blindness to the injustice of the situation and structures with which one is involved. Thus, the question of responsibility is generally both more complex and more subtle.

In traditional terms, there can be no discussion of personal responsibility and thus of personal sin, without the presence of knowledge and freedom. Therefore, where the blindness and lack of freedom of persons entangled in a sinful environment are significant, there can be no true sin for the individual. Clearly, however, the person would become culpable if and when he or she began to glimpse the reality of the situation and was free to respond. The scholastic tradition maintained further that people are responsible not only for actions which they perform but also for actions which they fail to perform, for sins of omission as well as commission; and thus, passivity in the face of a sinful situation may be as culpable as actions which perpetuate it.

It is clear that the excuse of ignorance should not be used too quickly to excuse persons who are unaware of injustices even though they are surrounded by the poor and the oppressed. Such ignorance is often, in Patrick Kerans' terms, "knowing ignorance."[16] Peter Henriot argues that the traditional doctrine of "inculpable ignorance" has often served to mask the presence of social sin: it is claimed that because the modern social scene is so complex, people cannot be held responsible for the structural roots of the injustices of the societies in which they live.[17]

As Bernard Häring points out, people are responsible for the development of their knowledge and freedom and cannot facilely claim either ignorance or powerlessness. People can be responsible for their own blindness to value when this blindness is a facile attempt to preserve their own privileges and position. Persons and groups can conceal the truth from themselves, often unconsciously, in order to preserve their own status or comfort. In this case the inability to perceive values flows from individual selfishness and sin.[18] They may be culpable where they fail to seek or respond to available information or accept uncritically the totality of the world-view offered by their culture and society. Though societal factors can cause a virtual blindness to value, this does not necessarily free the person of all responsibility for failing to perceive and strive to attain values.

Even in his early work, *The Law of Christ*,[19] Häring argued that ignorance can be virtually "pretended" (*ignorantia affectata*) when ignorance simply serves the purposes of the individual. Such ignorance would include varying degrees of sincerity and knowledge ranging from a sincere blind ignorance to "a calculating will which seeks the excuse of ignorance." Furthermore, knowledge is often hidden from those who refuse to make a reasonable and responsible effort to attain that knowledge. Responsibility for ignorance in this case is not less but actually more.[20]

In like manner, people can be responsible when their partial lack of freedom is the result of their own laziness, apathy, bad habits, and accumulated sinfulness.[21] Though the freedom of the human person is limited by social factors, it may also be limited and even lost through the failure of the individual. Häring refers to this as a "culpable loss or diminution" of freedom or a "sin against freedom."[22] In this situation the person is responsible for the loss or limitation of his or her freedom and the freedom of others due to apathy, inactivity, a failure to work to change the structure that is obstructing the growth of freedom. The individual is thus responsible for the unhealthy influence which these structures will exercise on himself or herself and on other men and women.

The difficulty of identifying the precise nature of personal responsibility for social sin has not led to an acceptance, at least in Roman Catholic theological circles, of any notion of "collective responsibility." Even those Roman Catholic theologians who advocate the development of a theology of

social sin are careful to repudiate any notion of collective guilt
or even the idea that structures or societies can—in the strict-
est sense—sin.[23] Baum states quite plainly that social sin
"produces evil consequences but no guilt in the ordinary
sense."[24] They stress, however, that it is necessary to widen the
understanding of personal responsibility beyond the simple
question of those acts performed by the individual with "full
knowledge and freedom."[25] In this regard Franz Böckle argues
that guilt is not simply an issue in individual morality; it is,
rather, "a collective political problem." The social extension
of guilt is founded on the fact that society itself "is an institu-
tionally structured multiplicity of individuals."[26]

Kenneth Himes, O.F.M., has provided a detailed and
helpful analysis of the problem of individual responsibility for
social sin.[27] Himes' analysis of the problem is structured on
distinctions among causal responsibility, moral responsibility
(culpability), and liability. The word "responsibility" carries
several possible meanings, two of which are most pertinent for
the discussion of social sin. The first meaning may be called
causal responsibility. This involves a non-moral or descriptive
assessment that one is the cause of an event—for example, his
comment was responsible for the laughter. The second meaning is not solely descriptive but evaluative and may be called
moral responsibility or culpability (blameworthiness). An example of the evaluative usage would be the statement "She is
the one responsible for starting the fight." "Liability," the
third distinct concept, attributes the requirement of making
some sort of restitution or reparation for evil committed or
damage done.

Actors may be held causally responsible even though
they lack the requirements of true moral agency. Thus, a
storm is causally responsible for a great deal of physical damage, human suffering and even death. In like manner, a social
group such as a corporation may be causally responsible for

the suffering inflicted on workers in a third world country. Moral responsibility or culpability, however, can only be attributed to true moral agents. It makes no sense to attribute moral blame to a storm; and, similarly, it makes no sense to attribute true moral blame to a collectivity such as a corporation. Himes thus rejects any notion of collective or corporate guilt. Rather, Himes argues, the attribution of true moral responsibility for social sin requires careful analysis of individual moral responsibility, an approach which he calls "distributive moral responsibility." Attribution of such individual culpability would require attention to such variables in each situation as causal responsibility, degree of voluntariness in cooperation, and the contributory role of the person in the evil perpetrated by the collective.

Liability is distinct from both causal and moral responsibility. It implies some moral requirement for restitution or reparation for an evil and cannot simply be identified with moral responsibility for the perpetration of the evil. Persons can be liable for evil consequences for which they bear no direct causal and thus no moral responsibility. Himes suggests that reparations paid to Japanese-Americans for wartime internment may be an example of such liability. The government officials presently in office and even a majority of tax payers who will indirectly pay the reparations bear no direct causal or moral responsibility for the evil perpetrated on Japanese-American citizens a generation ago.

Himes suggests, however, that liability may arise from the benefits and privileges which are afforded to individuals because of the past oppression of others, even where the privileged individuals did not cause nor approve of the evil. It might be argued that the disadvantage experienced by some white males as a result of affirmative action programs is not based on individual causal or moral responsibility for the past or present oppression of women and minorities in the workforce. Rather, these disadvantages may be justified by the privileges and benefits which white males experience in the workforce and in society in general precisely because of past injustices for which they bear no responsibility.

Himes offers an extremely useful analysis of the role of the individual in social sin. Yet, his analysis can seem to place greater emphasis on mitigating factors in determining individual responsibility to overcome social sin. Though Himes' line of argument clearly does not lessen the moral requirement of speaking out and working against injustice, by highlighting mitigating factors in assessing culpability it can seem to encourage complacency in the face of social sin. Some would argue, further, that his understanding of moral responsibility itself remains too narrow and individualistic. Considering the complex and dialectical relationship between individual and social group, it may be necessary to understand moral culpability and guilt in a broader perspective than the traditional discussion of individual knowledge and freedom as requirements for moral agency have allowed. While repudiating any concept of collective guilt in a strict sense, many theologians would suggest that personal responsibility, like personal freedom, always exists in a social context. Patrick McCormick argues that attention to individual culpability is suited to an understanding of sin as crime; but if sin is to be understood in a broader (social) context, then the concept of responsibility must follow suit.[28]

As was indicated in the beginning of the present section, efforts to identify personal responsibility for social sin and the appreciation of unavoidable participation in social sin is not meant to produce paralyzing guilt. People are limited in their ability to recognize injustice done to others by vast and complex systems. They are certainly limited in their ability to change these structures—even in concert with many other like-minded persons. Human persons are unavoidably limited in their ability to devote their energy to overcoming more than one or two oppressive situations at a time.

Yet, an awareness of social sin and our inevitable complicity in it does reduce the potential for self-satisfaction and confidence in one's state of moral purity. It would seem at the very least that the recognition of social sin necessitates a greater acceptance of self as sinner and a greater trust in God's mercy. It would also seem—almost inevitably—to create a constant inner tension which would challenge the sincere Christian to remain authentically and persistently committed to ongoing social transformation. As Rosemary Ruether points out, sinful structures remain a human creation which are perpetuated by the cooperation of men and women. Every effort must be made to unmask social sin, to disaffiliate from it, and to shape one's own attitudes and actions, as well as one's relationships, in a transformed and transformative way.[29]

# 5. Lonerganian Perspective on Social Sin

A distinct approach to a theology of social sin is offered by the work of theologians building on the cognitional theory and theological method of Bernard Lonergan.[1] The reflections of these theologians are by no means opposed to the theological and sociological foundations discussed thus far. In fact, Lonergan's cognitional theory is rather naturally concerned with topics of interest to the sociology of knowledge. Patrick Kerans' *Sinful Social Structures* already demonstrates the effort of relating the Lonerganian and sociological insights in constructing a theology of social sin.

Though not by any means incompatible with the work of other theologians reflecting on social sin, a Lonerganian approach remains distinct and seems to warrant separate discussion. This is the case not least because Lonergan's thought involves a distinct vocabulary and concepts. In fact, it is difficult to summarize the insights offered by theologians using a Lonerganian foundation since it is so dependent on the wider Lonerganian enterprise with its distinctive concepts and terminology. Thus, though an examination of Lonergan-inspired work is essential, more than a brief summary would be well beyond the scope of the present work.

## The Dynamics of Bias and Societal Decline

Of particular importance in developing a theology of social sin seems to be Lonergan's notion of "bias."[2] Bias is the human tendency to eliminate from consideration data upon which understanding, judgment, and decision will be based because the data is perceived to be a potential threat to our well-being or accustomed ways of viewing the world. But failure to account for significant data in this manner leads to a failure in human development since authentic self-transcendence requires the ability to challenge and transcend accustomed ways of viewing ourselves and the world. How Lonergan understands bias to arise need not concern the present discussion. Of greater significance for a theology of social sin is the fact that the manifestation and development of bias has profound effects on the individual and on society.

The effects of bias are both personal and social since they affect the direction of our own lives and the development of the environment in which others develop. To the extent that bias is reinforced by personal decision, the individual's freedom to live out his or her desires to know and love are circumvented. This, says Nancy Ring, is sin; and this sin establishes biases more firmly in the environment.[3]

Lonergan distinguishes four basic types of bias: dramatic bias, individual bias, group bias, and general bias. These biases are interrelated with one another, but of particular concern to a theology of social sin are group bias and general bias. The first type, dramatic bias, is the temptation to eliminate from the data upon which a decision will be made any affect which is painful or which offers some threat to the idealized picture of self operative in the person's imagination.

Individual bias is grounded in the force with which needs and desires are experienced by the individual. These needs and desires demand satisfaction with a force which seems to outweigh the needs of others and the common good. When this bias is followed, it leads to egoism, leaving the person short-sighted. By failing to look beyond immediately felt needs and desires, the individual frustrates the process by which he or she may learn the values embodied in culture and the good of order itself. Crime is the most obvious manifestation of the effects of individual bias.

Group bias is grounded in the decision-making of a group which has as its purpose the continued well-being of the group. This decision-making becomes biased when there is a refusal to consider the effects which such decisions may have on people who do not belong to that particular group and on other groups. Because individuals first receive their identities (through the process of "socialization")[4] from groups such as family, community, church, and nation, group bias easily leads to the creation of an environment in which others are implicated in the bias. It cuts off the development of creative ideas which are foreign and may seem to threaten the status of the group. When the interests of the dominant group are threatened, group bias functions to restrain the possibility of attending to the needs and desires of persons in other groups. Those in the dominant group become "blind" to the suffering of others and its causes and become unable to conceive of new possibilities for a more just social ordering.

Matthew Lamb discusses racism and sexism as examples of group bias. Racism, says Lamb, is rooted in the group bias by which persons are judged by superficial differences from the prevailing group. Racism in history has provided the biased excuse for the oppression and enslavement of other races and the colonial exploitation of nations and their resources.[5] Feminist theology emphasizes sexism as a form of "group egoism" by which both men and women are blinded to the possibilities for equal and mutual relationality.[6]

General bias, or "the general bias of common sense,"

refers to the impatience of common sense with anything which is not concrete and pragmatic. Common sense can become inflated so that human persons see only the immediate possibilities and courses of action. It resists the insights brought by more reflective thought as "merely" abstract or idealistic, and fails to be aware of the distortion already worked in the practical and pragmatic world which is the realm of common sense. Each group or society possesses its own common fund of conventional wisdom or commonsensical approach to the world. Thus, American and Japanese common sense differ. General bias resists recognition of any limitations in the group's common sense; it therefore resists change. In fact, it legitimates the distortions already produced by group bias.

We grow as individuals and groups precisely by admitting to our consciousness and decision-making all the data available at the moment. This requires a continuing effort to overcome the biases which tempt us to eliminate that data which seems to contain the possibility of threat—to ourselves or to our group. To the degree we choose to act within the narrow range of data offered by our biased perceptions or refuse to attempt to overcome the bias, we are engaged in sin. This sinful refusal and failure has profound individual and social ramifications.

The biases in interaction with one another prevent the development of society and the authentic self-transcendence of its members. Lonergan discusses this phenomenon as societal decline.[7] The biases have the power to distort social reality through the introduction of an element of irrationality into the social situation and into the historical process itself. This irrationality will take root in institutions resistant to any form of change, because the biases necessarily deflect implied and perceived threats to individual and group well-being. A defensiveness in the face of the perceived threat arises in persons and groups which further skews the social situation and its possibilities for authentic human development. Societies thus decline.

It is in this context, argues Kerans, that social structures can be said to be sinful.[8] They can be sinful in their source— as they emerge out of personal decisions which are biased, narrow, and destructive. They can be sinful in their conse- quences as other persons react defensively when confronted with structures which are sinful in their source. This further reinforces the destructive characteristics of the situation and creates an ongoing cycle of suspicion and defensiveness. Still others, powerless and thus unable to react defensively, will experience the sinful structures which they can neither oppose nor resist as oppressive and offensive to their human dignity.

## Lonergan and Social Conversion

It has been suggested that Bernard Lonergan's discussion of "bias" offers useful possibilities for furthering a theology of social sin. In light of these suggestions, it would seem that Lonergan's considerations of conversion and of bias might offer some useful insights for a developing theology of con- version as social. Some of these possibilities have already been suggested by those theologians who build on the work of Lonergan. In discussing Lonergan's notion of conversion, we anticipate the discussion of "social conversion," the subject of the following chapter.

The biases, as obstructions of authentic self-transcen- dence (whether religious, moral, affective or intellectual), can only be overcome through conversion. "Conversion," Lamb says, "is always a withdrawal from bias and sin; it is always a continuing transformation 'not yet' fully achieved."[9] More precisely it is the "praxis of agapic love" which breaks the hold of bias in the human heart and mind. This withdrawal from bias and social sin is accomplished only through ongoing and continuing effort—that is, by continual conversion.

In *Method in Theology*, Lonergan distinguishes three types of conversion: intellectual, moral, and religious.[10] Each is a type of self-transcendence.

> Intellectual conversion is a radical clarification and, consequently, the elimination of an exceedingly stubborn and misleading myth concerning reality, objectivity, and human knowledge. The myth is that knowing is like looking, that objectivity is seeing what is there to be seen and not seeing what is not there, and that the real is what is out there to be looked at. . . .
>
> Moral conversion changes the criterion of one's decisions and choices from satisfactions to values. . . . [It] consists in opting for the truly good, even for value against satisfaction when value and satisfaction conflict. . . .
>
> Religious conversion is being grasped by ultimate concern. It is other-worldly falling in love. It is total and permanent self-surrender without conditions, qualifications, reservations. But it is such a surrender, not as an act, but as a dynamic state that is prior to and principle of subsequent acts.

Nancy Ring suggests that it is primarily authentic moral conversion which overcomes individual and group bias. It does so through bringing the person to place values over satisfactions and through assisting the person in discerning satisfactions and needs which may be sacrificed for the good of others or for the common good. The general bias of common sense is overcome through intellectual conversion by showing the person that common sense can give insight into only one aspect of reality.[11] Lonergan himself maintains that it is one of the roles of religion to undo societal decline (which arises because of the biases) and promote societal progress through the promotion of self-transcendence.[12] Students of Lonergan's thought have identified Christian conversion as a specification of religious conversion. Christian conversion in particular, as that which gives unique shape to the other conversions, specifies the demands of moral conversion in terms of the neighbor and particularly of the poor, of victims.[13]

Conversion, for Lonergan, is not a solely private, individual phenomenon. He says of it:

> Conversion is existential, intensely personal, utterly intimate. But it is not so private as to be solitary. It can happen to many, and they can form a community to sustain one another in their self-transformation and help one another in working out the implications and fulfilling the promise of their new life. Finally, what can become communal, can become historical.[14]

The social and communal dimensions of conversion are further explicated by others building on Lonergan's thought. In rejecting any formulation of "first, then" in regard to personal conversion and social transformation, Walter Conn argues that ". . . society is not a collection of discrete individuals. Persons are social through and through; and society is personal. Private conversion is really no conversion. Authentic Christian conversion is fully personal; it is thus shaped by, and shapes, the structures of its social context."[15] Further, the community is necessary to encourage and sustain conversion and to carry out its implications in daily life.[16] Lamb, in particular, argues for the need for transformative communities to challenge biases.[17]

Lonergan's work is of course not without its critics. The present study cannot elaborate these in any detail. It is important to note, however, that some—notably Charles Davis[18]—have criticized Lonergan's work as being individualist and intellectualist. Davis argues that Lonergan offers a method for changing consciousness but not for changing society. He fails, says Davis, to recognize that knowing itself is a social activity and knowledge a social product. While Davis' critique is not without some merit, at least in the appearance which Lonergan's emphases may suggest, the critique does not seem entirely accurate—as the present chapter has attempted to demonstrate. In any case, it does not seem to negate the value of the Lonerganian perspective on the conversions and bias as they have been developed by theologians such as Lamb. Lamb, for example, argues that the overcoming of the biases as elements of social sin can only be overcome through "profound conversions of personal, social, cultural, economic, and political conduct or praxis."[19]

**Conclusion**

The cognitional theory of Bernard Lonergan adds distinctive and valuable perspectives on the problem of social sin. More specifically, it focuses more narrowly on how sin, through the phenomenon of bias, enters into human knowing. In this regard, Lonergan's philosophical discussion seems to coordinate well with the broader questions asked by the sociology of knowledge in regard to the social factors which influence human knowing. Thus, Lonerganian perspectives offer the possibility of examining how sin embodied in social structures influences the human person and is perpetuated in each person's understanding, judging, and deciding. It can then be seen how this process contributes to continuing societal decline, that is, to the ongoing oppression caused by social sin.

Likewise, Lonergan's very important discussion of conversion provides valuable insights into the possibilities of overcoming social sin. Its philosophical rather than sociological focus helps to examine more narrowly requirements for freeing oneself from the power of sin embodied in the societal institutions into which one is born and socialized. The next chapter will continue to examine how social sin can be overcome through conversion.

# 6. Social Conversion

Christian attention to sin is never an end in itself. Rather, sin must always be viewed within the context of the redemption from sin. Attention focused on personal sin alone involved a like focus on personal, individual salvation. A renewed appreciation of sin as a social reality must also involve a like focus on salvation as a social event. Jesus came to save individual persons in community. Just as Christians must not allow themselves to wallow in guilt over their personal sin, the subtle complexities of social sin must not cause the Christian to give up in powerless despair. The transition from sin to redemption involves conversion, whether from personal or from social sin; and yet, just as there is a problem in understanding the relationship of personal and social sin so too is there a problem in understanding the relationship of personal conversion and social transformation.

The present chapter will examine the effort to understand the transformation of social sin through "social conversion." First some remarks will have to be made concerning the shape of social conversion. Next the chapter will suggest some strategies for enabling a social conversion to occur. Thirdly, it will suggest some aspects of the church's distinctive mission in overcoming social sin. Finally, the chapter will examine the problem of the relationship between personal conversion and social transformation.

**The Shape of Authentic Social Conversion**

A number of theologians have suggested that conversion from social sin involves a new or renewed commitment to authentic community, to relationships with other persons which are free of oppression, injustice, and self-serving. Two symbols which are frequently suggested to denote the shape of this conversion from social sin are "community" and "solidarity."

Jerome Theisen has suggested that the appropriate verbal symbol for understanding sin is disunity.[1] The reality of sin involves multiple aspects of division and conflict in human existence. This involves personal disunity with self, others, and God which reaches its apex in a narcissistic self-centeredness. Sin also involves a broader disunity experienced when nations are in conflict, when one community oppresses another, when persons are alienated from the goods of the earth. Though Theisen's concern is focused especially on original sin as the precondition for moral evil, his reflections on sin as disunity offer some valuable insights for a theology of sin.

Theisen suggests further that the appropriate symbol for the reality of grace is community.[2] Community involves the overcoming of division and the dispelling of isolation. The community of the church is itself a symbol of the reality of grace bringing an end to disunity and a symbol of the eschatological community to be realized in the Age to come. Once again, Theisen's suggestion of "community" as a symbol for grace offers some valuable insights to an attempt to understand the transformation of social sin.

Similar reflections on renewed community are offered by feminist theologians as the shape of an authentic conversion. Sin, from a feminist perspective, involves a distorted relationality, translated into exploitation, perpetuated by social structures and false ideologies. Authentic conversion from this perspective involves a rejection of group egoism and the foundation of persons in an authentic community of equality and mutuality.[3]

Latin American liberation theologians develop similar insights in their reflection on the necessity for "solidarity"—solidarity first and foremost with the poor in their struggle for liberation against every sinful structure but also solidarity as the ultimate goal of human striving.[4] Solidarity is thus both the "key to conversion" from social sin and the ultimate aim of conversion. Though with different emphases and from a different perspective, Bernard Häring argues that "solidarity in sin" and the "sin of the world" must be overcome through conversion to an authentic "solidarity in salvation."[5] Pope John Paul II likewise suggests that "structures of sin" are overcome through the virtue of solidarity.[6] The pope understands solidarity to be "*a firm and persevering determination* to commit oneself to the *common good*" which is based on the conviction of the inherent relationship of all persons.

## Strategies for Conversion

Recognizing responsibility for sin, personal and social, leads the Christian to seek conversion. In fact, the recognition of sin is already the initial stage of the conversion process. It is a fundamental Christian affirmation that conversion always occurs by God's action and initiative. This occurs, however, with human cooperation; and, in fact, human effort can do much to pave the way for conversion and to enrich and solidify its effects. Here it will be possible to suggest only some of the more important aspects of strategies for a social conversion.

*A preferential option for the poor.* An important first step in seeking to lay the groundwork for a social conversion is the making of an "option for the poor." This option has been an important theme of Latin American liberation theologians who understand solidarity with the poor to be the only authentic starting point for theology. These theologians have helped to remind the Christian consciousness of God's action recalled in the Hebrew scriptures on behalf of the oppressed and marginalized, of the poor, of the alien and the widow and orphan. God's action on behalf of the poor is confirmed in Jesus who served the poor and the outcasts of his day and who challenged his disciples to follow his example.

The preferential option for the poor—for the economically deprived but also for all those who are oppressed and marginalized—has become a prominent theme in recent Catholic social ethics and teaching.[7] Looking at the world from the "underside," all people can be led to see the oppression caused by certain structures in the contemporary world. Working together with the poor, Christians can help empower them to become the agents of social transformation.

*Conscientization.* A second element of a strategy for social conversion, also prominent in liberation theology, is conscientization.[8] Most fundamentally, all people must come to a real appreciation of the dignity of all persons. More specifically, people must be awakened to the sin embodied in structures which is an affront to human dignity. The more fortunate must have their eyes opened to the suffering of the poor through education and through solidarity with the poor which will sensitize them to problems they face. The poor themselves must have their eyes opened to their own dignity and to the imperative that they become the principal participants in their own liberation. All people must become aware of the manner in which structures operate, in which they lend passive or active support to them, and in which evil becomes embodied in these structures.

*Social analysis.* In order for sinful structures to be overturned, these structures must be understood.[9] People hoping to bring about a social conversion must understand how injustice has come to be rooted in structures, how these structures work, and how they can best be overcome. They must be aware of the relationship between external structures such as political institutions and the internal structures which perpetuate injustice such as symbol and myth. Such an analysis must be particularly sensitive to the complex and intricate interaction of structures of different types—for example, the relationship of economic structures and political structures (i.e. how money "talks") and the relationship of political and religious structures (i.e. how religious symbols and myths can be used to legitimate political injustices). Failure to carry on this type of analysis will lead inevitably to short-lived solutions since the roots of the disease may still remain after its symptoms have been temporarily healed.

*Group/community action.* Social analysis of the complex structures of the contemporary world requires a good deal of cooperation among persons from different disciplines. These structures and their interaction are simply too complex to be understood when analyzed from only one perspective. Further, action against injustice and sin rooted in these complicated and entrenched structures must involve group action over time. Social structures are by nature resistant to change and thus efforts to overcome them must be persistent and carried on by groups. Examples of such groups would be political parties, labor unions, and churches and other religious organizations. Even more than groups, action to transform sinful social structures can best be carried on by communities, that is, people gathered together with a shared vision and organization. Such communities can be a source of challenge and support and collective action.

*Political action, conflict, and violence.* In democratic countries, efforts to overcome sinful social structures will generally entail political action. It is precisely through the political process that change can be brought about in many important areas of social concern, both nationally and internationally. Political involvement will necessarily involve conflict. In the context of genuinely democratic structures, such conflict is usually healthy and productive of realistic solutions to problems even where they must include compromise. In the face of repressive regimes or intransigent international structures, such conflict may seem to necessitate violence. This is especially the case when the oppression of the poor comes to be understood as a form of "institutionalized violence."[10] The Christian response to the important but difficult question of violence is clearly beyond the scope of the present discussion.

## The Special Mission of the Church

Virtually all of the strategies for social conversion mentioned above can be applied to the church's effort to bring about social transformation through overcoming social sin. The church does, however, have a distinctive manner of involvement in social involvement. In discussing social sin, Peter Henriot suggests that the church's involvement includes three important elements: the prophetic word, symbolic witness, and political action.[11] Building on the structure suggested by Henriot, we can suggest some elements of the church's distinctive mission.

*Prophetic word.* Drawing on the word of God contained in the scriptures, the church brings the message of the gospel to bear on every situation. In particular the church, from the perspective offered by God's word, has the critical function of challenging every situation of injustice and sin. It seeks to open the eyes of those blinded by social sin. Attending to the needs of those oppressed by sinful structures, analyzing the structural roots of their oppression, and drawing from the resources of its scriptures, the church challenges individual Christians and those outside the church to become aware of and to work to transform every structure which oppresses human dignity.

Particularly in light of its eschatological vision of the future made manifest in Jesus, the church critiques the present in light of the future. This future perspective gives the church some idea about the shape of the future hoped for. Further, the vision of the reign of God yet to be realized, together with the recognition that conversion is ultimately the work not of human effort but of grace, relativizes all present solutions and efforts. In this light, all present solutions, even those which seem the most just, must be seen as provisional and necessarily open to change. This relativizing action also has the effect of comforting Christians in the face of failure, offering them hope, and challenging them to find new ways to combat social sin. The vision of God's reign fully realized allows the church to seek reconciliation, not as a facile solution to present difficulty but as the goal of all efforts and as the context for the conflict necessary in order to bring about transformation.

*Symbolic witness.* In its own internal life, the church must make every effort to embody social conversion through structures and institutions which will serve justice and witness social conversion to all people.[12] Christians must strive to insure just external structures of organization with the church and just internal structures, that is, the authentic use of its myths and symbols in order to enhance justice. It must embody and teach authentic values to which wider society may be blind. The sacramental life of the church must witness the social nature of sin (especially in the sacrament of reconciliation) and the social nature of salvation (especially in the sacraments of reconciliation, baptism, and eucharist). The church must witness an effort to become involved, even at great cost, in efforts to confront and overcome every sinful social situation.

*Political action.* In order to effect change in the contemporary world, especially in democratic societies, it is imperative for the church to become involved in political action. Individual Christians must take their place in political office and in public policy discussion. The church as an institution must also enter into discussions about the formulation of just laws and just structures. Since the church has no "proper" mission in the social order,[13] it is necessarily limited in its ability to offer specific policy proposals with absolute assurance and to support particular political candidates; nonetheless, the mission of the Christian community to preach the good news of salvation necessarily involves attention to sinful structures which oppress persons and offend human dignity.

The U.S. bishops have taken an active part in attempting to influence public policy discussion in the United States.[14] This active role in American political discussion has always attempted to stop short of endorsing particular political parties or candidates. Further, the American bishops have explicitly recognized that sincere Catholics will inevitably disagree on particular political strategies.[15]

## Personal Conversion and Social Transformation

Social sin involves the embodiment of sin in social structures. These structures are the result of individual choices built up over time, but they gain an independence relative to human choice. Structures exercise an influence on human persons, for good or ill, even though they are unaware of their power. Because of the complexity and subtle power of structures, it may seem therefore that in order for social sin to be overturned structures must first be changed. Once the unjust structures are overturned people may be sufficiently free of their influence to effect an authentic personal conversion.

On the other hand, it seems apparent that structures themselves cannot be overturned—at least in any lasting manner—without changing persons. Even if one could change every unjust structure, if one did not simultaneously change the hearts of men and women they would eventually rebuild the old structures of injustice or develop new and more resilient ones. Social sin exercises its influence not only exteriorly but also interiorly. Structures may be transformed but the attitudes and worldviews, the ideologies and blindnesses, which produced and sustained them would still remain.

It would seem clear that two extreme positions in the possible understanding of the relationship of personal conversion and social conversion must be rejected: on the one hand, the pietistic claim that personal conversion must come first and social transformation will necessarily follow; and, on the other hand, the Marxist claim that overturning unjust structures will bring about a change of heart. The truth seems to lie somewhere between these two extremes: somehow there is a simultaneity between personal conversion and social transformation. As there is a dialectical relationship between person and society, personal and social sin, so there exists a dialectical relationship between personal and social conversion.[16]

Jürgen Moltmann has called the belief that personal transformation can occur without a change in circumstances and structures "an idealist illusion" which seems to imply that the human person is a soul without a body. On the other hand, the effort to transform external circumstances without inner transformation is "a materialist illusion" that seems to suppose that human persons are products of social circumstances and nothing else.[17] The practical necessity of this simultaneity is confirmed by the theological affirmation that salvation itself is both personal and social.

The logical necessity for simultaneity in social and personal transformation does not imply that in different situations, temporal priority may have to be given to one or the other. Juan Segundo, while rejecting any general notion of the priority of personal conversion, argues that it is obvious that personal conversion must come temporally first for those who are to work for social transformation in order that others may be converted.[18] In some situations, unjust structures may be so firmly entrenched that the effort to overturn them in the present may cause greater harm than good. In such a situation, the effort to bring individual persons to conversion may be the most prudential initial course. On the other hand, some structures may be so great an affront to human dignity and to human life itself that they can no longer be tolerated. To work for their transformation may be a clear moral requirement in the present despite the obstacles and foreseeable consequences. Though temporal priority may have to be given to either personal or social transformation in a particular situation, it must be recalled that ultimately both must be accomplished together. Failure to recognize this fact will almost necessarily result in a short-circuiting of any long-term hopes for transformation.

Recent statements of the Roman Catholic bishops of the United States have been criticized for placing too much emphasis on structural change and not enough on changing human hearts.[19] Liberation theologians and Latin American bishops are also criticized for the same emphasis, though the Medellín documents may be used to indicate a different perspective: "The uniqueness of the Christian message does not so much consist in the affirmation of the necessity for structural change as it does in the insistence on the conversion of men which, in turn, will bring about this change."[20]

A slightly different perspective yet is offered by the statement from the 1971 Bishops' Synod—"Action on behalf of justice and participation in the transformation of the world fully appear to us as a constitutive dimension of the preaching of the Gospel, or, in other words, of the Church's mission for the redemption of the human race and its liberation from every oppressive situation."[21] Many commentators on this crucial statement argue that if its challenge is taken seriously, then action on behalf of justice—social transformation—can in no way be secondary to personal conversion.[22] If the gospel is to be preached authentically, then evangelization must be accompanied by action for justice and participation in efforts to transform the world and to liberate persons from every oppressive situation. The implication that logical priority cannot be given either to personal conversion or to social transformation seems clear.

### Conclusion

The Christian tradition always understands sin, social or personal, within the context of the redemption from sin accomplished by God in Jesus Christ. The present chapter has addressed the shape of social conversion and the question of individual responsibility for social sin. It has attempted to suggest some strategies for attaining this conversion.

# Conclusion

The fact that sin must be understood as a social reality
has become generally accepted in Roman Catholic theology.
The present work has attempted to provide a critical overview
of theological reflection on social sin. And yet, the theology of
social sin is in need of further development especially in the
effort to clarify its theological and sociological foundations. In
part, the work which remains is part of the ongoing effort of
Catholic theology to arrive at a renewed understanding of sin
in general. Current discussion of social sin has attempted to
incorporate biblical perspectives and sociological insight, but
this effort needs continuing attention. As previous chapters
have suggested, further to be incorporated are insights from
Lonergan's cognitional theory and notion of conversion as
well as the feminist emphases on the mythic, symbolic, and
linguistic roots of social sin.

Perhaps a greater challenge is the effort to move the discussion of social sin out of the arena of theory and the world
of academia into the critical consciousness of the Christian
community. Since it seems probable that most Catholics still
consider sin to be a personal matter, this educational task
remains almost monumental; and yet, if as Christians we are
to understand the nature of the sin which we renounce and
oppose, then we must understand that it is much broader and

more complex than our own individual sin. The message of God's liberating action in Jesus is not fully understood unless it is seen that salvation is broader than my individual salvation from my individual sin.

Furthermore the message of social sin and social conversion must be preached in such a way as to challenge sincere Christians to action rather than to inflict paralyzing or discouraging guilt. It is a painful experience to realize that one is implicated, even indirectly, in the suffering of other persons. Obviously the attempt to open the eyes of those implicated in social sin will cause resentment in those who already have a vague awareness of the threat which social transformation raises to their own comfort and prerogatives. The message of Jesus meets resistance in the hearts even of the most sincere, so that authentic conversion always involves the painful realization of one's sin and the painful struggle to leave aside old and comfortable ways. Still, the effort to educate and preach about social sin must not alienate sincere Christians unnecessarily since this would be counterproductive to the transformation which such education and preaching attempts to encourage. Sin, both social and personal, must always be understood within the broader context of God's redeeming action in Christ and Christ's victory over sin.

Perhaps the greatest challenge of the theology of social sin is the challenge to conversion itself, individual and communal. To call on the mercy of God in Jesus Christ is to renounce all sin, personal and social—that is, my own individual sinful acts and attitudes and life's direction as well as any complicity with sinful structures which oppress other persons. To become a follower of Jesus is to oppose sin in all its forms and manifestations—in my own acts, attitudes and relationships and in the world around me. To gather as church is to commit ourselves to be an authentic witness to God's liberating action through the lifestyle and structures and institutional priorities of the Christian community. The message of an authentic theology of social sin is only of value if it challenges and enables people to the conversion of their own lives and to the ongoing transformation of the world.

# Notes

## Introduction

1. Karl Menninger, *Whatever Became of Sin?* (New York: Hawthorn, 1973).

## Chapter 1

1. For an overview of the history of the theology of sin, see Henri Rondet, *The Theology of Sin*, trans. Royce W. Hughes (Notre Dame: Fides, 1960). Also useful, but more uneven, is Pietro Palazzini and Salvador Canals, ed., *Sin, Its Reality and Nature: An Historical Survey*, trans. Brendan Devlin (Dublin: Scepter, 1964).

2. See, for example, Eugene H. Maly, *Sin: Biblical Perspectives* (Dayton, OH: Pflaum/Standard, 1973), esp. pp. 17–22; and Alphonse Spilly, "Sin and Alienation in the Old Testament: The Personalist Approach," *Chicago Studies* 21 (Fall 1982): 211–25.

3. There seems to be little dispute among biblical scholars concerning the fact that Gen 3–11 displays the effects of sin in various social relationships. Some dispute, however, the contention that these chapters are meant to show a process of the *growth* of sin. See, for example: Claus Westermann, *Genesis 1–11: A Commentary*, trans. John J. Scullion (Minneapolis: Augsburg, 1984).

4. R. B. Y. Scott, *The Relevance of the Prophets*, rev. ed. (New York: Macmillan, 1967), pp. 180–85. See also James Limburg, *The*

*Prophets and the Powerless* (Atlanta: John Knox, 1977), especially chapter 5 (pp. 54–75) which offers a useful analysis on the prophet Amos and the affluent society of his day.

5. Jerome Murphy-O'Connor, *Becoming Human Together* (Wilmington, DE: Michael Glazier,1977), pp. 81–102. See also Rudolf Schnackenburg, *The Moral Teaching of the New Testament* (New York: Seabury, 1973), pp. 278–86.

6. Raymond E. Brown, *The Gospel According to John (I-XII)*, The Anchor Bible, vol. 29 (Garden City, NY: Doubleday and Company, 1966), pp. 508–10.

7. See Norbert J. Rigali, "Sin in a Relational World," *Chicago Studies* 23 (November 1984): 321–32; Bernard Häring, *Sin in the Secular Age* (Garden City, NY: Doubleday, 1974), esp. pp. 106–34.

8. Patrick Kerans, *Sinful Social Structures* (New York: Paulist, 1974) p. 58; Gregory Baum, *Religion and Alienation: A Theological Reading of Sociology* (New York: Paulist, 1975), pp. 198–99.

9. Patrick McCormick, *Sin as Addiction* (New York: Paulist, 1989), pp. 54–75.

10. Rigali, pp. 322–24.

11. See Leonardo Boff, *Liberating Grace*, trans. John Drury (Maryknoll, NY: Orbis, 1979).

12. Heribert Jone and Urban Adelman, *Moral Theology* (Westminster, MD: Newman, 1958), p. 46.

13. Henry Davis, *Moral and Pastoral Theology*, vol. 1, 6th ed. (London: Sheed and Ward, 1949), p. 203.

14. Thomas F. Schindler, *Ethics: The Social Dimension*, Theology and Life series, vol. 27 (Wilmington, DE: Michael Glazier, 1989), pp. 129–30. See also Peter J. Henriot, "The Concept of Social Sin," *Catholic Mind* 71 (October 1973): 41–42; and Henriot, "Social Sin: The Recovery of a Christian Tradition," in *Method in Ministry: Theological Reflection and Christian Ministry*, ed. James D. Whitehead and Evelyn Eaton Whitehead (New York: Seabury), pp. 133–35.

15. For early works reflecting this shift in the theology of sin, see Piet Schoonenberg, *Man and Sin: A Theological View*, trans.

Joseph Donceel (Notre Dame: University of Notre Dame Press, 1965); Louis Monden, *Sin, Liberty and Law*, trans. Joseph Donceel (New York: Sheed and Ward, 1965); and later, Bernard Häring, *Sin in the Secular Age* (Garden City, NY: Doubleday, 1974).

16. See especially Paul Ricoeur, *The Symbolism of Evil*, trans. Emerson Buchanan (Boston: Beacon, 1967).

17. Henriot, "The Concept of Social Sin," pp. 39–47.

18. Henriot, "Concept of Social Sin," p. 43; "The Recovery," p. 136. See also Paul Bock, *In Search of a Responsible World Society: The Social Teachings of the World Council of Churches* (Philadelphia: Westminster, 1974), esp. pp. 81–88.

19. Henriot, "The Concept of Social Sin," pp. 42–47.

20. *Gaudium et spes* in Joseph Gremillion, *The Gospel of Peace and Justice: Catholic Social Teaching since Pope John* (Maryknoll, NY: Orbis, 1976), p. 263.

21. Ricardo Antoncich, *Christians in the Face of Injustice: A Latin American Reading of Catholic Social Teaching*, trans. Matthew J. O'Connell (Maryknoll, NY: Orbis, 1987), pp. 4–11. See also Henriot, "The Recovery," pp. 141–42.

22. 1971 Synod of Bishops, *Justice in the World*, in Gremillion, p. 514.

23. Ibid., in Gremillion, p. 524.

24. Ibid., in Gremillion, p. 525.

25. Pope John Paul II, *Reconciliation and Penance* (Washington: USCC, 1984), #16, pp. 50–56. For commentary and critique, see Norbert Rigali, "Human Solidarity and Sin in the Apostolic Exhortation, *Reconciliation and Penance*," *The Living Light* 21 (June 1985): 337–44.

26. Pope John Paul II, *On Social Concerns* (Dec. 30, 1987), Pt. V, #35–39 (Washington: USCC, 1988), pp. 67–78.

27. Dorothee Soelle, *Political Theology*, trans. John Shelley (Philadelphia: Fortress, 1974), esp. ch. 7: "Sin, Politically Interpreted," pp. 83–92.

28. See Charles Davis, "Theology and Praxis," *Cross Currents* 23 (Summer 1973): 154–68.

29. Gustavo Gutiérrez discusses three levels in the meaning of

the term "liberation." *A Theology of Liberation*, trans. Sr. Caridad Inda and John Eagleson (Maryknoll, NY: Orbis, 1973), pp. 36–37, 176–78.

30. Rosemary Radford Ruether, *Sexism and God-Talk: Toward A Feminist Theology* (Boston: Beacon, 1983), esp. pp. 159–92.

31. Many of these articles will be cited in discussions to follow.

32. *Sharing the Light of Faith: National Catechetical Directory for Catholics in the United States* (Washington: USCC, 1979), art. 165b. See also the official commentary on the Directory: *Sharing the Light of Faith: An Official Commentary* (Washington: USCC, 1981), pp. 69–70.

33. See James E. Hug, "Social Sin, Cultural Healing," *Chicago Studies* 23 (November 1984): 333–34. Hug notes that interest in a theology of social sin has waned significantly since the mid-1970s, except in "social action circles and liberation theologies" (p. 334). A brief search for articles on social sin since that time would seem to confirm Hug's assertion.

34. Henriot, "The Concept of Social Sin," pp. 41–42; "The Recovery," pp. 133–35.

35. That personal sin has social effects was recently reaffirmed by Pope John Paul II in *Reconciliation and Penance*, esp. #15, pp. 48–50.

36. Rigali, "Human Solidarity and Sin," p. 344.

37. *Reconciliation and Penance*, #16, pp. 53–54. See also Rigali, "Human Solidarity and Sin," 337–44.

38. Pope John Paul II, *On Social Concerns*, #36, p. 69.

39. Mark O'Keefe, O.S.B., "An Analysis and Critique of the Social Aspects of Sin and Conversion in the Moral Theology of Bernard Häring" (S.T.D. dissertation, The Catholic University of America, 1987).

40. Many of the theologians who propose to understand sin as *both* personal and social will be cited in the pages which follow. Many of these discussions refer directly or indirectly to the work of Paul Ricoeur, *The Symbolism of Evil* (Boston: Beacon, 1967). Orlando E. Costas argues that the very dichotomy between personal and social sin, between personal and social salvation, is both sense-

less and false. Costas, *Christ Outside the Gate: Mission Beyond Christendom* (Maryknoll, NY: Orbis, 1982), pp. 37–38.

41. Ricoeur, pp. 309–15.

42. George J. Dyer, "The Other Dimension," *Chicago Studies* 23 (November 1984): 241.

43. Kerans, pp. 78–79.

44. Ibid., p. 59.

45. Schindler, p. 140.

46. Ruether, *Sexism and God-Talk*, p. 181.

47. Rosemary Radford Ruether, "Feminist Theology and Spirituality," in *Christian Feminism: Visions of a New Humanity*, ed. Judith L. Weidman (San Francisco: Harper and Row, 1984), pp. 25–26.

48. Kerans, p. 51. See also: Baum, *Religion and Alienation*, p. 197; and McVerry, "Sin: The Social, National, and International Aspects," *Way Supplement* 48 (Fall 1983): 41–42.

49. Baum, *Religion and Alienation*, pp. 203–205.

50. Pope John Paul II, *Reconciliation and Penance*, #16, pp. 50–55. The Congregation for the Doctrine of the Faith, though recognizing the evil which is embodied in social, economic, and political structures, emphasizes that all evil is rooted ultimately in the human heart—from human knowledge and freedom. See: CDF, "Instruction on Certain Aspects of the 'Theology of Liberation'" (Washington: USCC, 1984), #14–15, p. 12.

51. McCormick, pp. 101–102.

52. In the first chapter (pp. 1–12), McCormick discusses the value of analyzing models of sin and the interrelation of model to model. The other chapters lay out the shape of each model.

53. The approach to sin in terms of freedom and knowledge is a distinctively, though not exclusively, Catholic one. It would be interesting to compare Catholic views on social sin with those offered by Protestant theologians, based on their differing views on sin in general.

A recent "debate" in the pages of *The Ecumenist* between theologians Gregory Baum and Darrol Bryant seems to exemplify the differing emphases in Roman Catholic and Protestant theologies of sin which result in differing perspectives on a notion of

"social sin." *The Ecumenist* 21 (May-August 1983): 49–54
[Bryant], 54–60 [Baum]; 22 (January-February 1984): 20–23
[Bryant], 23–24 [Baum]. Reflections on the debate are offered by:
Douglas Webster, "The Debate on Social Sin Continues," *The
Ecumenist* 22 (January-February, 1984): 17–20; and Martin
Rumscheidt, "Redeemed from the Bondage of Sin," *The Ecumenist* 22 (March-April 1984): 33–35.
  54. Schindler, pp. 129–49.
  55. Ibid., p. 140.
  56. Ibid., p. 142.
  57. Ibid., p. 143.


**Chapter 2**

  1. Piet Schoonenberg, *Man and Sin* (Notre Dame: University
of Notre Dame Press, 1965).
  2. O'Keefe, dissertation, 1987.
  3. Bernard Häring, *This Time of Salvation*, trans. Arlene
Swidler (New York: Herder and Herder, 1966), p. 230.
  4. Bernard Häring, *Free and Faithful in Christ: Moral Theology for Clergy and Laity* (New York: Seabury, 1981), 3:167–69.
  5. *Sin in the Secular Age*, pp. 110–11, 124. Schoonenberg (pp.
124–25) develops the same distinction: *peccatum originale originatum* being "passive original sin . . . a sinful state which affects man
from his origin" and *peccatum originale originans* being "that fact
which caused everybody to enter the world with passive original sin
. . . that is, the fall." Schoonenberg seems more willing than Häring,
however, to equate "the sin of the world" with "passive original
sin" (pp. 179–80). See also Jerome P. Theisen, *Community and
Disunity: Symbols of Grace and Sin* (Collegeville, MN: St. John's
University Press, 1985), pp. 58–59.
  6. "The Concept of Social Sin," pp. 40, 47–48; "The Recovery," pp. 128–29; "Social Sin and Conversion: A Theology of the
Church's Involvement," *Chicago Studies* 11 (Summer 1972):
120–21. In each case, Henriot offers helpful concrete examples.
  7. Baum, *Religion and Alienation*, pp. 200–203.

8. *Sharing the Light of Faith: An Official Commentary*, p. 70.

9. Baum, p. 200.

10. Schindler, p. 142.

11. Ibid., p. 140.

12. Kerans, p. 79.

13. William J. Byron, *Toward Stewardship: An Interim Ethic of Poverty, Power, and Pollution*, Topics in Moral Argument (New York: Paulist, 1975), p. 47.

14. McVerry, p. 39.

15. McCormick, p. 120.

16. Michael Novak, "Structures of Virtue, Structures of Sin: A Theology of Natural Liberty," *America* 160 (Jan. 28, 1989): 54–60.

17. See, for example, Elisabeth Schüssler Fiorenza, "Breaking the Silence—Becoming Visible," in *Women: Invisible in Church and Theology*, ed. Elisabeth Schüssler Fiorenza and Mary Collins, Concilium: Religion in the Eighties, 182 (Edinburgh: T. and T. Clark, 1985), pp. 3–16. For a more expansive and radical discussion of patriarchal structures, see Mary Daly, *Gyn/Ecology: The Metaethics of Radical Feminism* (Boston: Beacon, 1978).

18. "Partners in the Mystery of Redemption: First Draft of United States Bishops' Pastoral Response to Women's Concerns for Church and Society," *Origins* 17 (April 21, 1988), pp. 757–88, esp. #39–43, #224–25, pp. 763–64, 781.

19. Ruether, "Feminist Theology and Spirituality," pp. 16–27; and *Sexism and God-Talk*, pp. 165–73.

20. Elisabeth Schüssler Fiorenza, *In Memory of Her: A Feminist Theological Reconstruction of Christian Origins* (New York: Crossroad, 1983).

21. In discussing "structures of sin," Pope John Paul II identifies two of the "most typical" *attitudes* which undergird these sinful structures: "all-consuming desire for profit" and "the thirst for power." *On Social Concerns*, #37, p. 71.

22. Kerans, pp. 62–65.

23. Ricoeur, pp. 151–57; discussed by Kerans, pp. 65–68. See also McCormick, pp. 107–10.

24. Kerans, pp. 101–104.

25. Soelle, pp. 89–92.

26. Kerans, pp. 68–79. The suggestions for a theology of social sin which may flow from a Lonerganian perspective will be discussed in a later chapter.

27. Ibid., pp. 83–104.

28. Häring, *Free and Faithful in Christ*, 1:387–88.

29. *Man Becoming: God in Secular Language* (New York: Herder and Herder, 1970), pp. 118–26. See also: Henriot, "The Concept of Social Sin," p. 52.

30. Ibid., pp. 121–22.

31. Häring, *This Time of Salvation*, pp. 231–35.

32. *Reconciliation and Penance*, #14, p. 47. The pope cites Rom 7:7–25 and Eph 2:2; 6:12.

33. The social implications of the Pauline metaphor "principalities and powers" is nicely spelled out in David G. Buttrick, *Preaching Jesus Christ: An Exercise in Homiletic Theology* (Philadelphia: Fortress, 1988). For a further discussion of a Pauline understanding of sin, see Jerome Murphy-O'Connor, *Becoming Human Together* (Wilmington, DE: Michael Glazier, 1977).

34. McCormick, pp. 110–45.

35. Ibid., pp. 146–77.

36. James E. Hug, "Social Sin, Cultural Healing," *Chicago Studies* 23 (November 1984): 333–51.

37. Bernard Häring, *The Healing Power of Peace and Nonviolence* (New York: Paulist, 1986).

38. McCormick, pp. 178–200.

## Chapter 3

1. Henriot, "The Concept of Social Sin," p. 43. Patrick McCormick (pp. 90–95, 117–18) notes that the effort to use sociology in understanding the relationship between the individual and the social world parallels recent efforts of psychology and psychiatry to identify the social "evils" which interrelate with individual psychopathologies. Family therapy, especially therapy with the families of alcoholics, focuses on analyses of familial relationships and sys-

tems. Diagnosis and treatment involve attention not only to the individual patient but to the "social system" within which the patient operates.

2. The precise manner in which the social sciences are to be used in theological method—particularly in moral theological method—remains somewhat problematic. For example, considering the vastness and variety of social scientific disciplines, it is difficult for theologians to incorporate sociological data without being ideologically selective. The problems involved, however, in no way mitigate the importance of the effort.

3. Peter L. Berger and Thomas Luckmann, *The Social Construction of Reality: A Treatise on the Sociology of Knowledge* (New York: Doubleday, 1966; Anchor Books, 1967). The work of Berger and Luckmann is, of course, not without its critics. See, for example, Peter Hamilton, *Knowledge and Social Structure: An Introduction to the Classical Argument in the Sociology of Knowledge* (London: Routledge and Kegan Paul, 1974), pp. 137–46.

4. Pope John XXIII, *Mater et Magistra* (1961), in Gremillion, pp. 143–99.

5. Häring, *Free and Faithful in Christ*, 1:90–101.

6. Berger and Luckmann, p. 61.

7. Henriot, "The Concept of Social Sin," pp. 49–50; "The Recovery," p. 130.

8. Ibid., p. 50.

9. Berger and Luckmann, pp. 88–92.

10. Joe Holland and Peter Henriot, S.J., *Social Analysis: Linking Faith and Justice*, rev. ed. (Maryknoll, NY: Orbis, 1983), esp. pp. 21–30.

11. Byron, p. 45.

12. Ibid., pp. 45–46. Byron argues, by way of example, that the American economic and social system is not basically evil but structural reform is required in order to facilitate the empowerment of the poor.

13. See, for example, Häring's *Macht und Ohnmacht der Religion: Religionssozologie als Anruf* (Salzburg: Otto Müller, 1956), pp. 82–86; *Christian Renewal in a Changing World*, trans. M. Lu-

cinda Häring (New York: Desclée, 1964), pp. 64–67; and *Morality is for Persons: The Ethics of Christian Personalism* (New York: Farrar, Straus, and Giroux, 1971), pp. 59–86.

14. Bernard Häring, *What Does Christ Want?* (Staten Island, NY: Alba House, 1968), p. 206.

15. Häring, *Morality is for Persons*, p. 77.

16. Schoonenberg, pp. 104–106.

17. Kerans, pp. 73–76.

18. In addition to the work of Berger and Luckmann, see also the very readable Peter A. Berger, *Invitation to Sociology: A Humanistic Perspective* (Garden City, NY: Doubleday/Anchor, 1963). Obviously, sociology has continued to advance since the work by Berger and his collaboration with Luckmann; and yet these works are most frequently cited by proponents of a theology of social sin. It seems likely that the present development of this theology does not require entering into the subtleties of sociological argument.

19. Schüssler Fiorenza, "Breaking the Silence," pp. 11–13.

20. Häring, *Free and Faithful in Christ*, 1:265–70.

21. Bernard Lonergan, referring to the thought of Max Scheler, maintains that the rejection of one particular value can result in a distortion of the whole scale of values in an individual, group, or even an epoch. Lonergan, *Method in Theology* (New York: Herder and Herder, 1972), p. 33.

22. Berger and Luckmann, pp. 72–79.

23. McCormick, pp. 116–17.

24. Bruce C. Birch and Larry L. Rasmussen, *Bible and Ethics in the Christian Life*, rev. ed. (Minneapolis: Augsburg, 1989), pp. 70–99.

25. See Paulo Freire, *Pedagogy of the Oppressed*, trans. Myra Bergman Ramos (New York: Herder and Herder, 1972); and his more recent *The Politics of Education: Culture, Power, and Liberation*, trans. Donaldo Macedo (South Hadley, MA: Bergin and Garvey, 1985).

26. Peter C. Hodgson, *New Birth of Freedom: A Theology of Bondage and Liberation* (Philadelphia: Fortress, 1976).

27. Kerans, p. 7.

## Chapter 4

1. Karl Rahner, "Reflections on the Unity of the Love of Neighbor and the Love of God," in *Theological Investigations* VI, trans. Karl-H. and Boniface Kruger (New York: Crossroad, 1982), pp. 231–49. See also Rahner, *The Love of Jesus and the Love of Neighbor*, trans. Robert Barr (New York: Crossroad, 1983), esp. pp. 63–104.

2. Richard M. Gula, S.S., *Reason Informed by Faith: Foundations of Catholic Morality* (New York: Paulist, 1989), pp. 100–101.

3. Ruether, *Sexism and God-Talk*, esp. pp. 72–92.

4. Baum, *Religion and Alienation*, pp. 203–204.

5. Grace as "mediated" is a traditional principle of Roman Catholic theology which does not seem to be explicitly mentioned by Häring in the context of his discussions of the social aspects of sin and conversion. Cf. Boff, *Liberating Grace* (Chap. 13: "The Social Structure of Habitual and Actual Grace"), pp. 141–47.

6. James L. O'Connor, "Original Sin: Contemporary Approaches," *Theological Studies* 29 (June 1968): 230.

7. Häring, *Sin in the Secular Age*, p. 87; and *Free and Faithful in Christ*, 1:151–52.

8. *Free and Faithful*, 1:389.

9. *What Does Christ Want?*, p. 208.

10. *Gaudium et spes*, no. 25, in Gremillion, p. 263.

11. Häring, *Sin in the Secular Age*, p. 87; and *Free and Faithful*, 1:151–52.

12. National Conference of Catholic Bishops, "Brothers and Sisters to Us: A Pastoral Letter on Racism," in *Quest for Justice*, ed. J. Brian Benestad and Francis J. Butler (Washington, DC, 1981), pp. 375–76.

13. "The 'Sin of the World' and Normative Morality," in *Personal Responsibility and Christian Morality*, pp. 153–75.

14. Fuchs, p. 160.

15. Curran discusses his "theology of compromise" in a number of his writings: *Critical Concerns*, p. 93; *Themes in Fundamental Moral Theology* (Notre Dame, IN: University of Notre Dame Press, 1977), pp. 139–44; *Ongoing Revision in Moral Theology*

(Notre Dame, IN: Fides/Claretian, 1975), pp. 182–90; *Catholic Moral Theology in Dialogue* (Notre Dame, IN: University of Notre Dame Press, 1972), pp. 184–219; and *A New Look at Christian Morality* (Notre Dame, IN: Fides, 1968), pp. 169–73.

16. Kerans, pp. 100–101.

17. Henriot, "The Concept of Social Sin," p. 42.

18. *Sin in the Secular Age*, p. 83.

19. Bernard Häring, *The Law of Christ: Moral Theology for Priests and Laity*, trans. Edwin C. Kaiser from the 5th German ed., 3 vols. (Westminster, MD: The Newman Press, 1963–66).

20. Ibid., 1:108–13.

21. Bernard Häring, *Shalom: Peace. The Sacrament of Reconciliation*, rev. ed. (Garden City, New York: Doubleday/Image, 1969), pp. 293–94.

22. See, for example: *Sin in the Secular Age*, pp. 135–36, 165–68; and *Free and Faithful*, 1:262–63.

23. The Protestant theologian of liberation Orlando Costas, drawing from examples in the Old Testament and from Pauline letters, does speak both of "corporate sin" and of "collective guilt." *Christ Outside the Gate*, pp. 25–26. It may be that differing Protestant perspectives on sin in general may lead to differing perspectives on the question of collective guilt. See also the "debate" between Bryant and Baum in *The Ecumenist* 21–22.

24. Baum, p. 200. Curran makes a similar statement: "But the sin of the world refers to the sinful structures and realities present in our world and in no way to personal guilt, blame or responsibility." *Critical Concerns*, p. 95. These statements of Baum and Curran taken alone seem to over-simplify a complex problem.

25. Kerans, p. 58; Baum, p. 200; Franz Böckle, *Fundamental Moral Theology*, trans. N.D. Smith (New York: Pueblo, 1977), p. 104.

26. Böckle, p. 75.

27. Kenneth Himes, OFM, "Social Sin and the Role of the Individual," *Annual of the Society of Christian Ethics* (1986): 183–218.

28. McCormick, pp. 138–43. See also Schindler, pp. 142–46.

29. Ruether, *Sexism and God-Talk*, p. 182.

## Chapter 5

1. See, for example, William P. Loewe, "Dialectics of Sin: Lonergan's *Insight* and the Critical Theory of Max Horkheimer," *Anglican Theological Review* 61 (1979): 224–45; Kerans, *Sinful Social Structures*; Matthew Lamb, *Solidarity with Victims*; Nancy C. Ring, "Sin and Transformation from a Systematic Perspective," *Chicago Studies* 23 (1984): 303–19.

2. See especially: Lonergan, *Insight: A Study of Human Understanding* (London: Longmans, Green and Co., 1957; reprint ed., New York: Harper and Row, 1978), pp. 218–42.

3. Ring, p. 313.

4. Kerans, pp. 76–77.

5. Lamb, pp. 5–7.

6. Ruether, *Sexism and God-Talk*, p. 164.

7. *Insight*, pp. 218–42; *Method*, pp. 52–55, 117.

8. Kerans, pp. 77–79.

9. Lamb, p. 10.

10. *Method*, pp. 238–40. Lonergan was criticized for failing to take adequate account of human affectivity in his account of conversion. See: Robert M. Doran, "Psychic Conversion," *The Thomist* (April 1977): 200–36. This criticism has led many theologians influenced by Lonergan to add "affective" conversion to the religious, moral and intellectual conversions identified by Lonergan in *Method*.

11. Ring, pp. 317–18.

12. *Method*, p. 55.

13. Walter Conn, *Christian Conversion: A Developmental Interpretation of Autonomy and Surrender* (New York: Paulist, 1986), p. 203; Lamb, p. 13.

14. *Method*, p. 130.

15. Conn, pp. 204–205. See also: Gustavo Gutiérrez, *A Theology of Liberation*, p. 205.

16. See, for example: Conn, p. 134. See also: Rosemary Haughton, *The Transformation of Man* (Springfield, IL: Templegate, 1967; reprint, 1980), pp. 153–280.

17. Lamb, p. 12.

18. Charles Davis, "Lonergan's Appropriation of the Concept of Praxis," *New Blackfriars* 62 (1981): 114–26.

19. Lamb, p. 120.

## Chapter 6

1. Theisen, *Community and Disunity*, esp. pp. 53–83.

2. Ibid., esp. pp. 87–130.

3. Ruether, *Sexism and God-Talk*, pp. 164, 183–92.

4. Jon Sobrino and Juan Hernández Pico, *Theology of Christian Solidarity*, trans. Phillip Berryman (Maryknoll, NY: Orbis, 1985.)

5. Häring, *Free and Faithful in Christ*, 1:129–31. See also O'Keefe dissertation.

6. Pope John Paul II, *On Social Concern*, #38–40, pp. 72–80.

7. See, for example, Pope John Paul II, *On Social Concern*, #42, pp. 84–85. See also Donal Dorr's commentary on Catholic social teaching: *Option for the Poor: A Hundred Years of Vatican Social Teaching* (Maryknoll, NY: Orbis, 1983).

8. See Paulo Freire, *Pedagogy of the Oppressed*; and Letty M. Russell, *Human Liberation in a Feminist Perspective—A Theology* (Philadelphia: Westminster, 1974), pp. 66–67, 113–17.

9. Especially helpful is Holland and Henriot, *Social Analysis* (Maryknoll, NY: Orbis, 1983).

10. Medellín documents, "Peace," #16, in Gremillion, p. 460.

11. Henriot, "Social Sin and Conversion," pp. 122–30.

12. *Justice in the World*, #39–48, in Gremillion, pp. 522–23.

13. *Gaudium et spes*, #42, in Gremillion, p. 276.

14. See, for example, the documents collected in J. Brian Benestad and Francis J. Butler, eds., *Quest for Justice: A Compendium of Statements of the United States Catholic Bishops on the Political and Social Order 1966–80* (Washington: USCC, 1981).

15. USCC Administrative Board, "Political Responsibility: Choices for the Future," *Origins* 17 (Nov. 5, 1987): 370–75.

16. Ruether, "Feminist Theology and Spirituality," pp. 25–26.

17. Jürgen Moltmann, *The Crucified God*, trans. R.A. Wilson and John Bowden (London: SCM Press, 1974), p. 23.

18. Juan Luis Segundo, S.J., *Evolution and Guilt*, A Theology for Artisans of a New Humanity, vol. 5, trans. John Drury (Maryknoll, NY: Orbis, 1974), pp. 68–69.

19. J. Brian Benestad, *The Pursuit of a Just Social Order: Policy Statements of the U.S. Catholic Bishops, 1966–80* (Washington, DC: Ethics and Public Policy Center, 1982), pp. 93–118.

20. Medellín documents, "Justice," #3 in Gremillion, p. 447. Recent documents from the official magisterium continue to emphasize the priority of personal conversion. See, for example: Sacred Congregation for the Doctrine of the Faith, "Instruction on Certain Aspects of the 'Theology of Liberation'," #8–9, pp. 31–32; Pope John Paul II, *Reconciliation and Penance*, #16, pp. 55–56; and Congregation for the Doctrine of the Faith, "Instruction on Christian Freedom and Liberation," #75, March 22, 1986 (Washington: USCC, 1986), p. 45.

21. "Justice in the World," #6 in Gremillion, p. 514.

22. See, for example: Richard McBrien, "The Church and Social Change: An Ecclesiological Critique," in *Theology Confronts a Changing World*, ed. Thomas M. McFadden (West Mystic, CT: Twenty-Third Publications, 1977), pp. 44–62; and Charles M. Murphy, "Action for Justice as Constitutive of the Preaching of the Gospel: What Did the 1971 Synod Mean?" *Theological Studies* 44 (June 1983): 298–311.

# Bibliography

Baum, Gregory. *Religion and Alienation: A Theological Reading of Sociology.* New York: Paulist Press, 1975.

Berger, Peter L. and Luckmann, Thomas. *The Social Construction of Reality.* New York: Doubleday, 1966.

Bryant, Darroll. "Should Sin Be Politicized?" *Ecumenist* 21 (May-August 1983): 49–54.

Reply by Gregory Baum, *Ecumenist* 21 (May-August 1983): 54–60.

Response by Bryant, *Ecumenist* 22 (January-February 1984): 20–23.

Reflection on the debate by Baum, *Ecumenist* 22 (January-February 1984): 23–24.

Byron, William J. *Toward Stewardship: An Interim Ethic of Poverty, Power and Pollution.* Topics in Moral Argument. New York: Paulist, 1975.

Dyer, George J. "The Other Dimension." *Chicago Studies* 23 (November 1984): 241–59.

Fiorenza, Elisabeth Schüssler. "Breaking the Silence—Becoming Visible." In *Women: Invisible in Church and Theology*, pp. 3–16. Edited by Elisabeth Schüssler Fiorenza and Mary Collins. Concilium 182. Edinburgh: T. and T. Clark, 1985.

Fuchs, Josef. "The 'Sin of the World' and Normative Morality." In *Personal Responsibility and Christian Morality*, pp. 153–75. Translated by William Cleves et al. Washington, DC: Georgetown University Press, 1983.

Gutiérrez, Gustavo. *A Theology of Liberation*. Translated by Sr. Caridad Inda and John Eagleson. Maryknoll, NY: Orbis, 1973.

Häring, Bernard. *Free and Faithful in Christ: Moral Theology for Clergy and Laity*. 3 vols. New York: Seabury, 1978–81.

———. *Sin in the Secular Age*. Garden City, NY: Doubleday, 1974.

Henriot, Peter. "The Concept of Social Sin." *Catholic Mind* 71 (October 1973): 38–53.

———. "Social Sin and Conversion: A Theology of the Church's Involvement." *Chicago Studies* 11 (Summer 1972): 115–30.

———. "Social Sin: The Recovery of a Christian Tradition." In *Method in Ministry: Theological Reflection and Chris-*

*tian Ministry*, pp. 127–44. Edited by James D. Whitehead and Evelyn Eaton Whitehead. New York: Seabury,
1980.

Himes, Kenneth R. "Social Sin and the Role of the Individual." *Annual of the Society of Christian Ethics* (1986):
183–218.

Hodgson, Peter C. *New Birth of Freedom: A Theology of
Bondage and Liberation*. Philadelphia: Fortress, 1976.

Holland, Joe and Henriot, Peter. *Social Analysis: Linking
Faith and Justice*. Rev. ed. Maryknoll, NY: Orbis, 1983.

Hug, James E. "Social Sin, Cultural Healing." *Chicago Studies* 23 (November 1984): 333–51.

John Paul II. *Reconciliation and Penance*. Apostolic Exhortation. (December 2, 1984) Washington: USCC, 1984.

———. *On Social Concerns*. Encyclical letter. (December 30,
1987) Washington: USCC, 1988.

Kerans, Patrick. *Sinful Social Structures*. New York: Paulist
Press, 1974.

Lamb, Matthew. *Solidarity with Victims: Toward a Theology
of Social Transformation*. New York: Crossroad, 1985.

Loewe, William P. "Dialectics of Sin: Lonergan's *Insight* and
the Critical Theory of Max Horkheimer." *Anglican
Theological Review* 61 (April 1979): 224–45.

Lonergan, Bernard J.F. *Insight: A Study of Human Under-*

*standing*. London: Longmans, Green, and Co., 1957; reprint ed., New York: Harper and Row, 1980.

———. *Method in Theology*. New York: Herder and Herder, 1972; reprint ed., New York: The Seabury Library of Contemporary Theology, 1979.

McCormick, Patrick. *Sin as Addiction*. New York: Paulist, 1989.

McVerry, Peter. "Sin: the Social, National, and International Aspects." *Way Supplement* 48 (Fall 1983): 39–49.

Murphy-O'Connor, Jerome. *Becoming Human Together*. Dublin: Veritas, 1978.

Novak, Michael. "Structures of Virtue, Structures of Sin: A Theology of Natural Liberty." *America* 160 (January 28, 1989): 54–60.

Ricoeur, Paul. *The Symbolism of Evil*. Translated by Emerson Buchanan. Boston: Beacon Press, 1967.

Rigali, Norbert. "Human Solidarity and Sin in the Apostolic Exhortation, Reconciliation and Peace." *Living Light* 21 (June 1985): 337–44.

———. "Sin in a Relational World." *Chicago Studies* 23 (November 1984): 321–32.

Ring, Nancy C. "Sin and Transformation From a Systematic Perspective." *Chicago Studies* 23 (November 1984): 303–19.

Ruether, Rosemary Radford. "Feminist Theology and Spirituality." In *Christian Feminism: Visions of a New Humanity*, pp. 9–32. Edited by Judith L. Weidman. San Francisco: Harper and Row, 1984.

——. *Sexism and God-Talk: Toward a Feminist Theology.* Boston: Beacon, 1983.

Schindler, Thomas F. *Ethics: The Social Dimension. Individualism and the Catholic Tradition.* Theology and Life series, vol. 27. Wilmington, DE: Michael Glazier, 1989.

Schoonenberg, Piet. *Man and Sin: A Theological View.* Translated by Joseph Donceel. Notre Dame, IN: University of Notre Dame Press, 1965.

Segundo, Juan Luis. *Evolution and Guilt.* Translated by John Drury. A Theology for Artisans of a New Humanity, vol. 5. Maryknoll, NY: Orbis, 1974.

——. *Grace and the Human Condition.* Translated by John Drury. A Theology for Artisans of a New Humanity, vol. 2. Maryknoll, NY: Orbis, 1973.

Soelle, Dorothee. *Political Theology.* Translated by John Shelley. Philadelphia: Fortress, 1974.

Theisen, Jerome P. *Community and Disunity: Symbols of Grace and Sin.* Collegeville, MN: St. John's University Press, 1985.